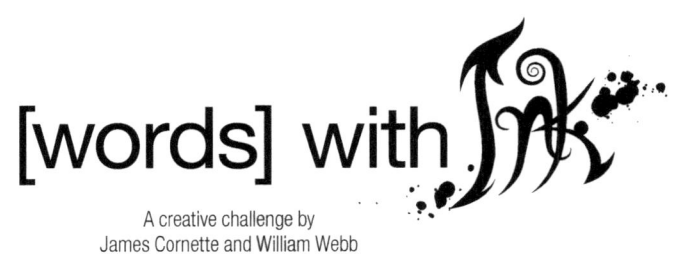

A creative challenge by
James Cornette and William Webb

Words with ink began as a personal project between Bill Webb and James "Cornfu" Cornette to encourage creativity and habit building. We would alternate turns passing a word to each other to illustrate over the course of a week. One person would illustrate while the other person took a break.

The hidden gem of this project was to see how each artist would visually define the word. It was about pushing each other to be more creative on how we would interpret words while honing drawing skills.

Bill and I decided not to be restrictive on the medium used. I opted for going digital and used a cintiq. Bill went with markers and ink. Working in a comfortable medium allowed for focus on the illustration and not the tools.

Our combined efforts are within the following pages. Bill and I hope you enjoy viewing the art as much as we did creating it and that you are motivated to start your own creative project.

Make stuff!
Cornfu

CHALLENGE WORDS

for cornfu:
tyrant
raijin
marauder
juggernaut
cryptic
malediction
paladin
carnival
morning star
speed
containment
lunar
behemoth

for bill:
bounty hunter
shovel monkey
king
destroyer
whiplash
vengeance
abaddon
rabbit samurai
pack
courage
kamaitachi
robot
bloat

01 CHALLENGE WORD:
tyrant

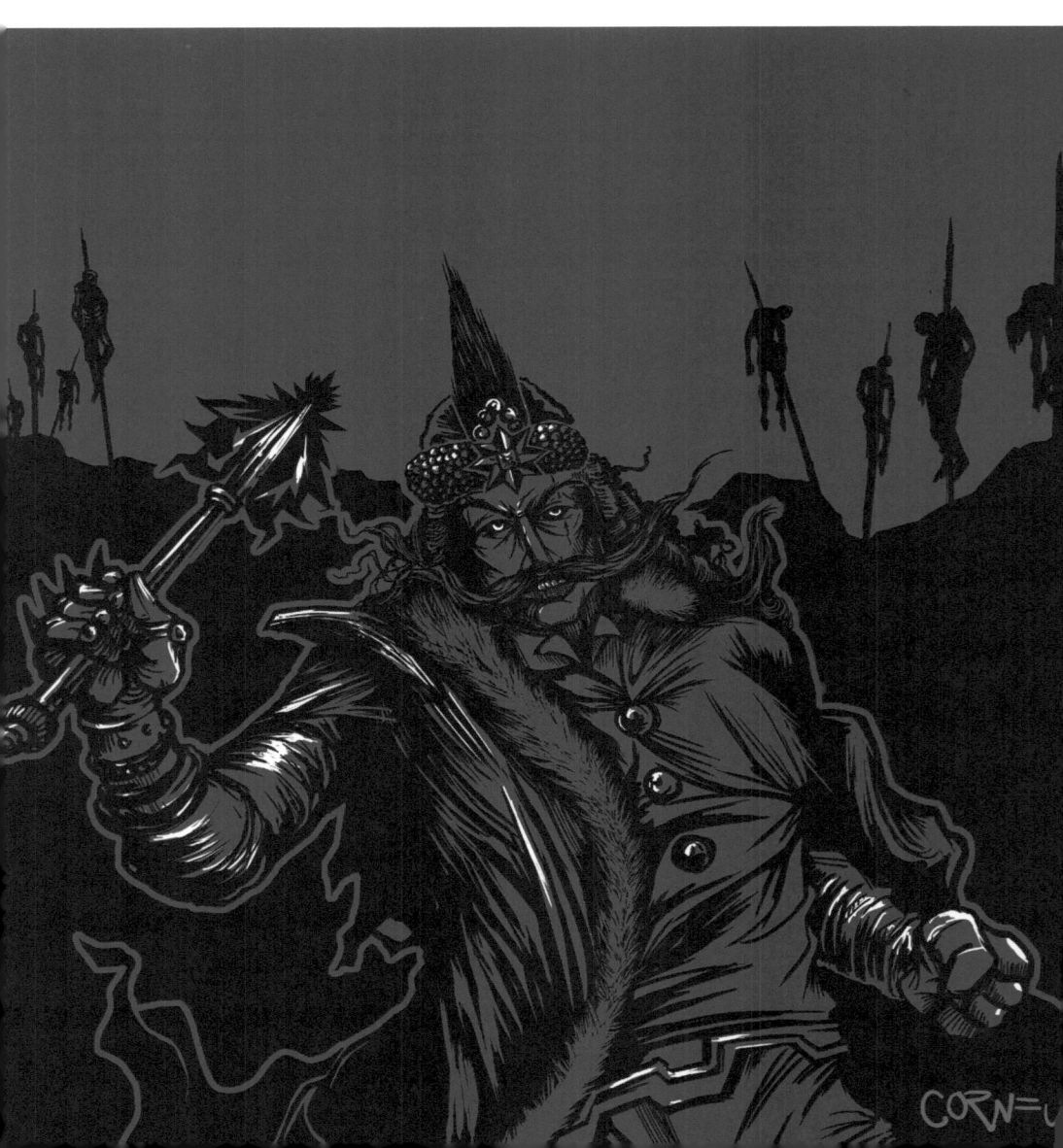

01 CHALLENGE WORD:
bounty hunter

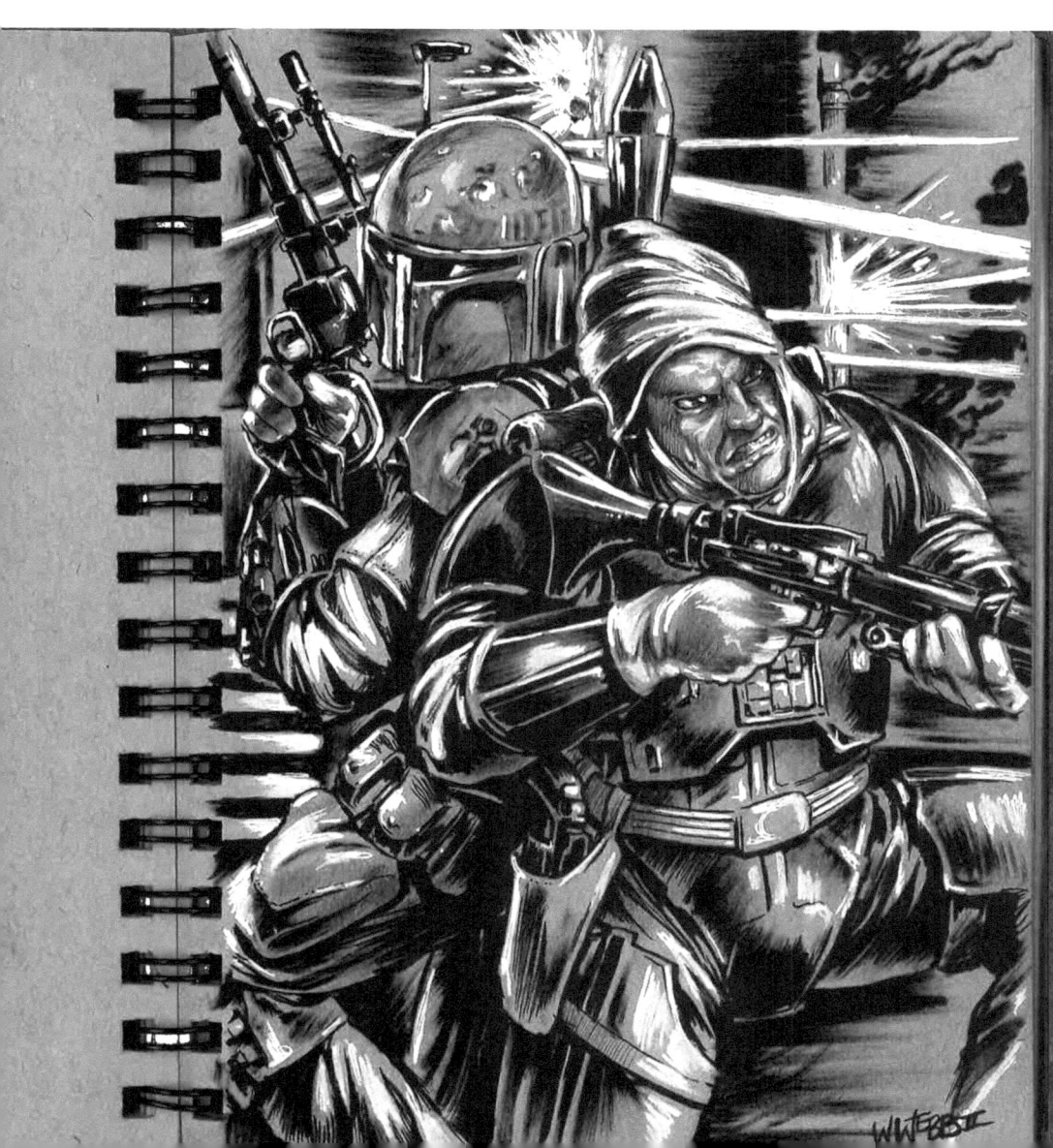

02 CHALLENGE WORD:
raijin

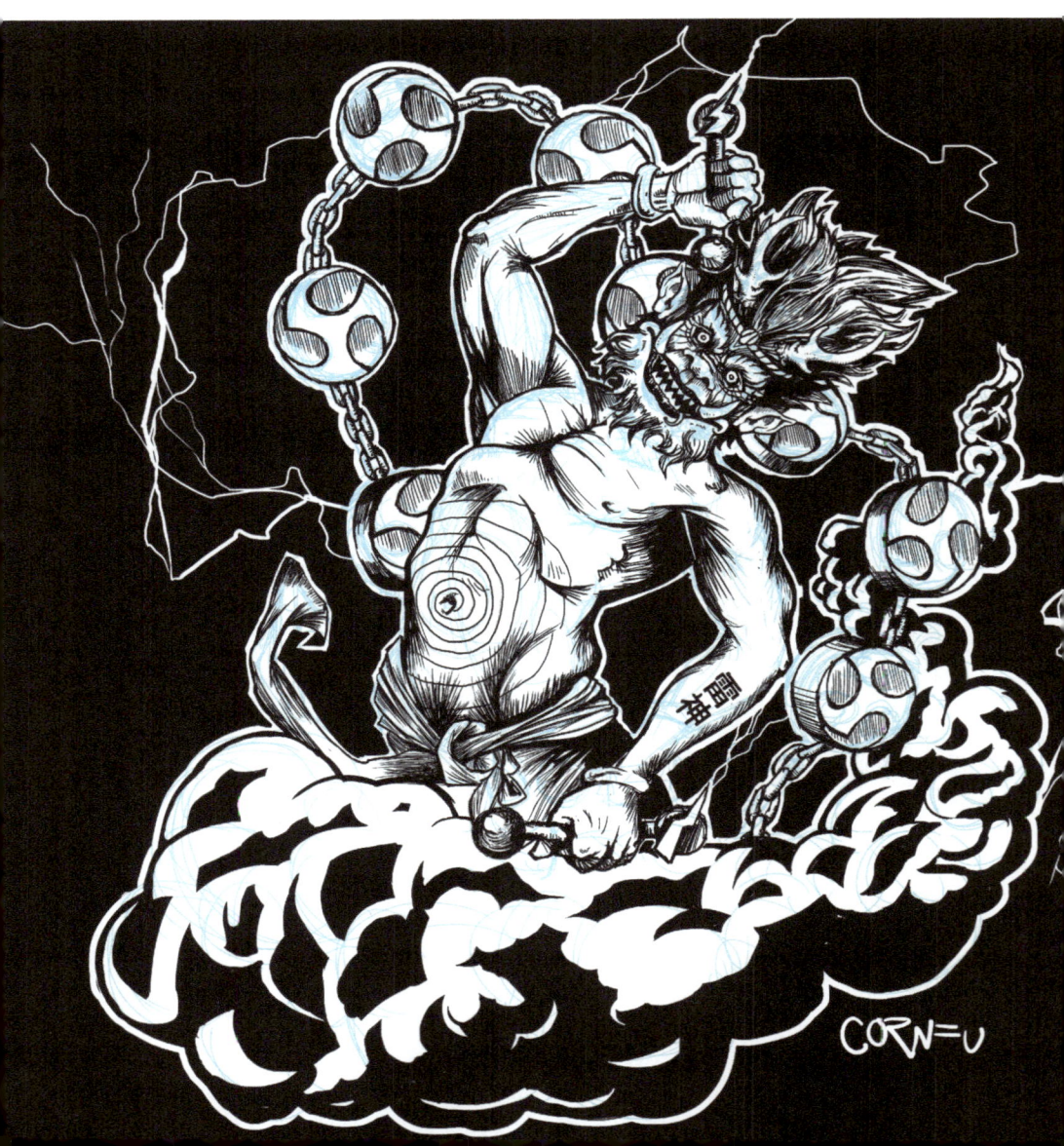

02 CHALLENGE WORD:
shovel monkey

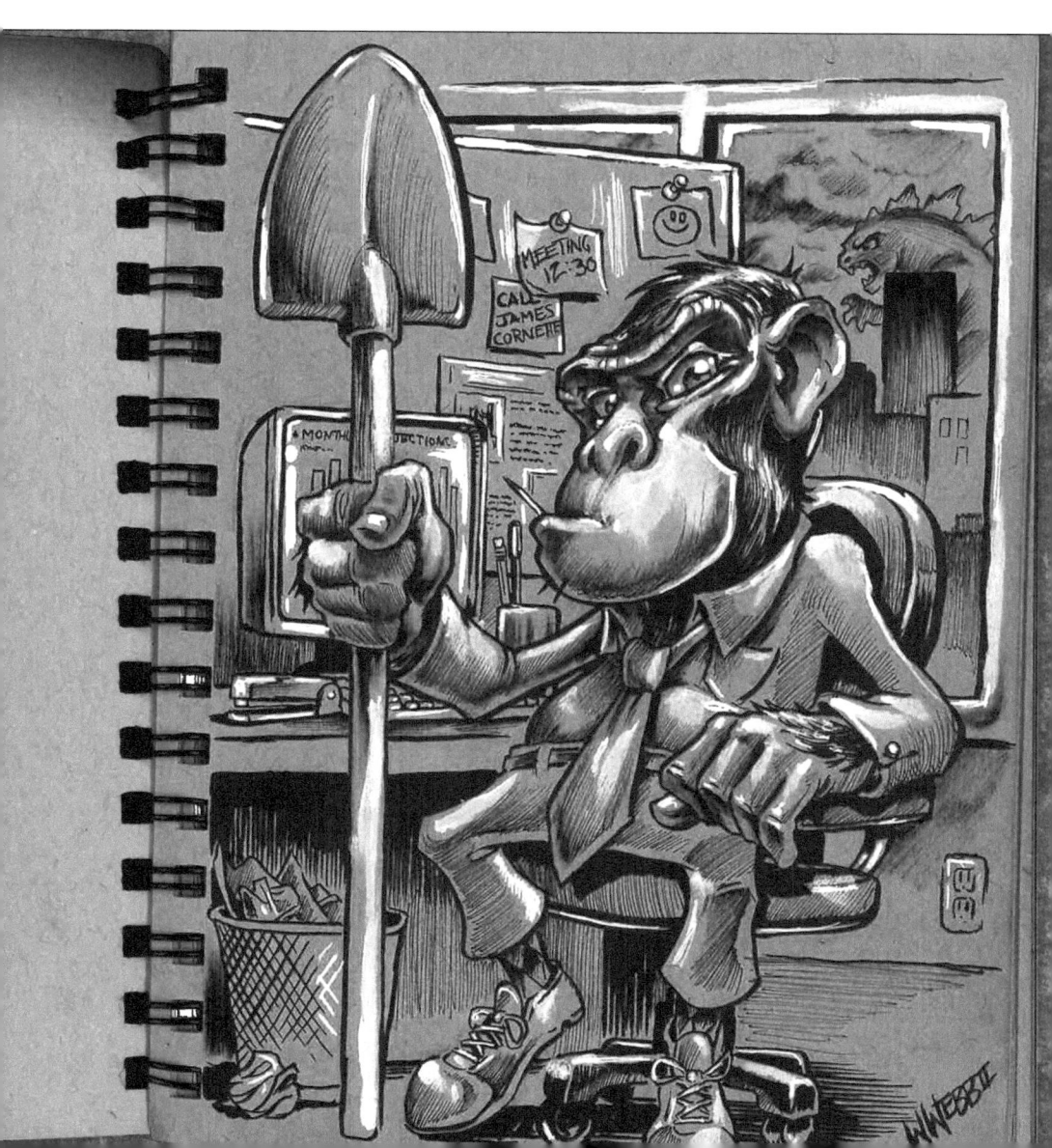

03 CHALLENGE WORD:
marauder

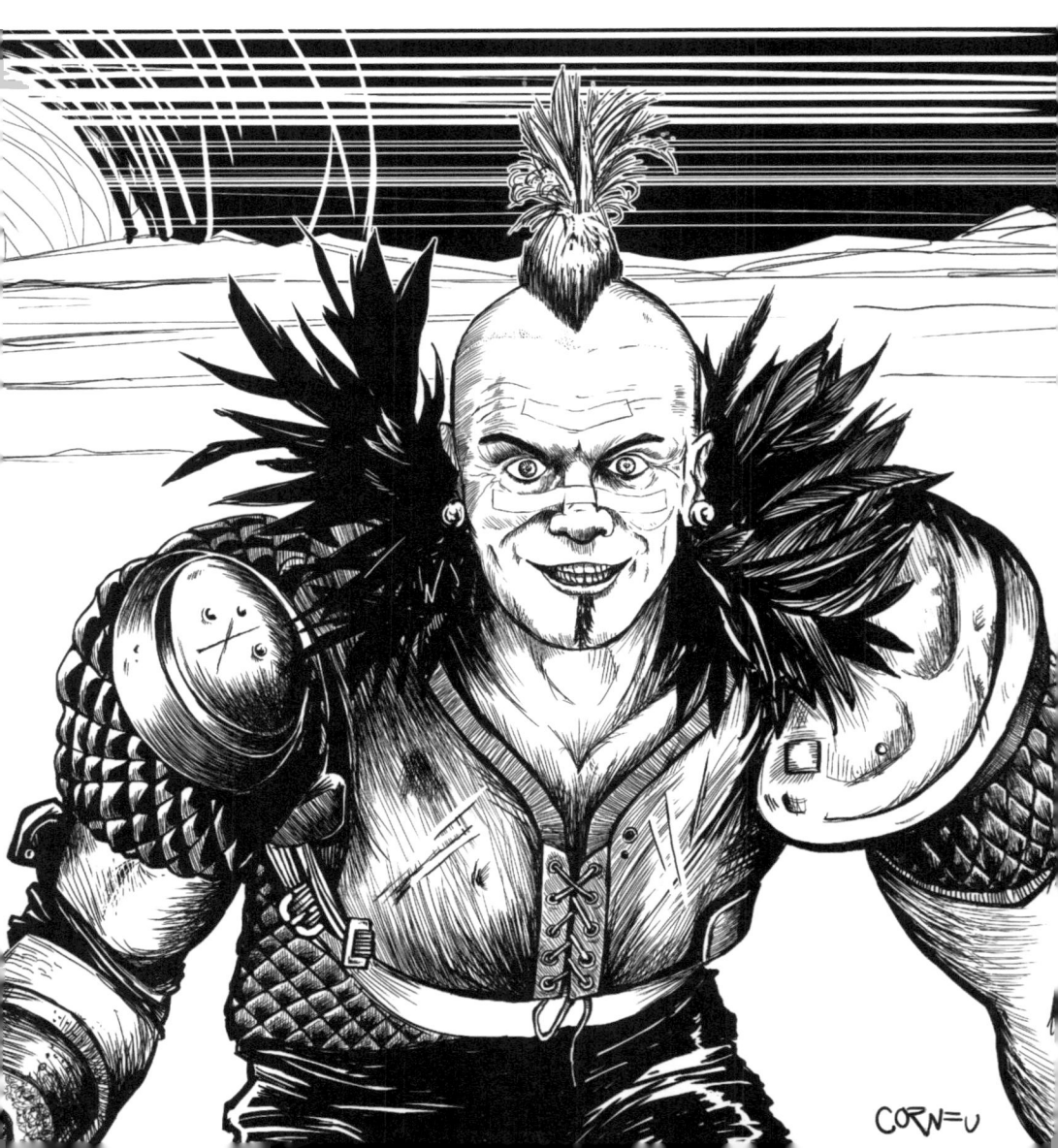

03 CHALLENGE WORD: king

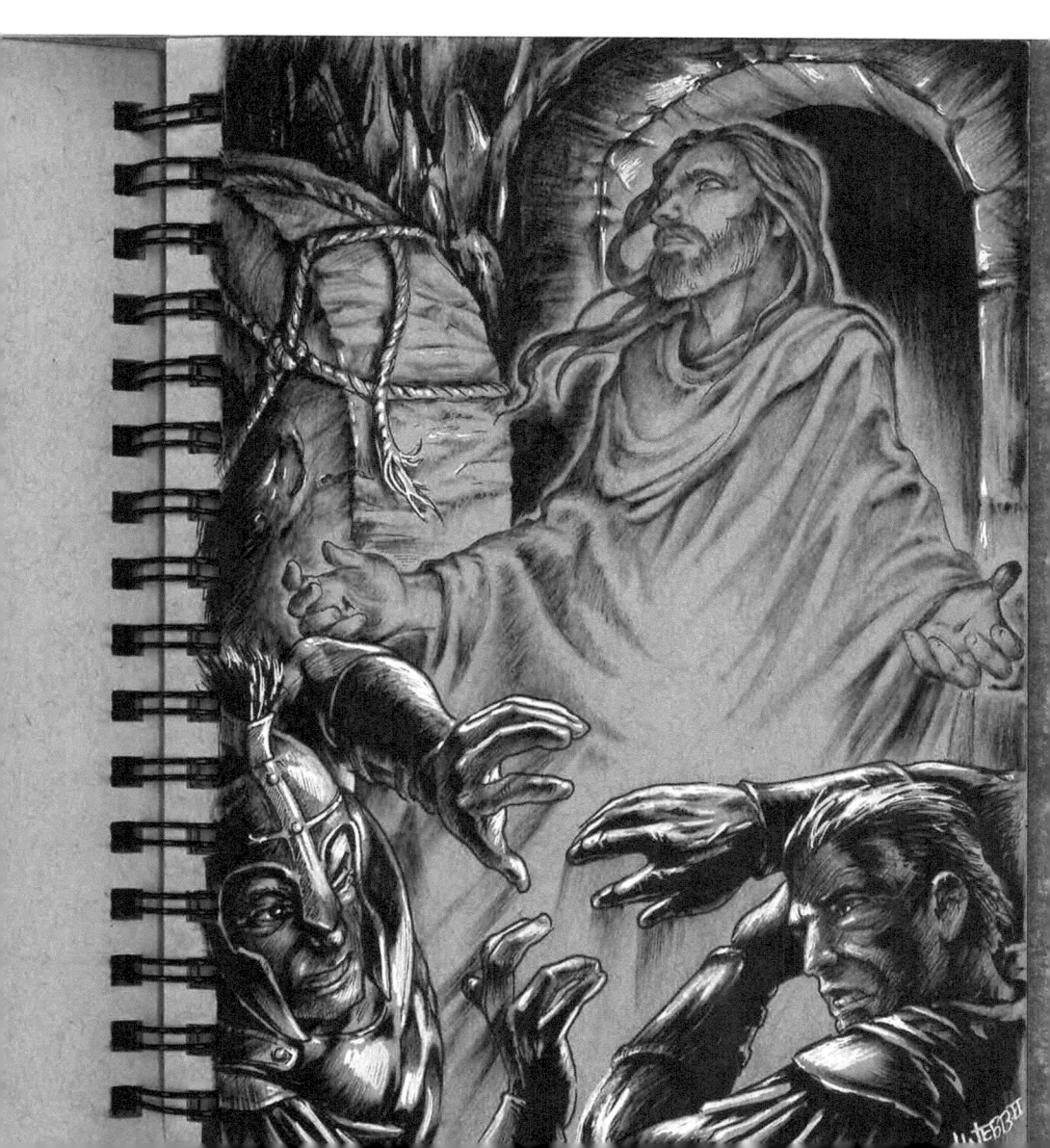

04 CHALLENGE WORD:
juggernaut

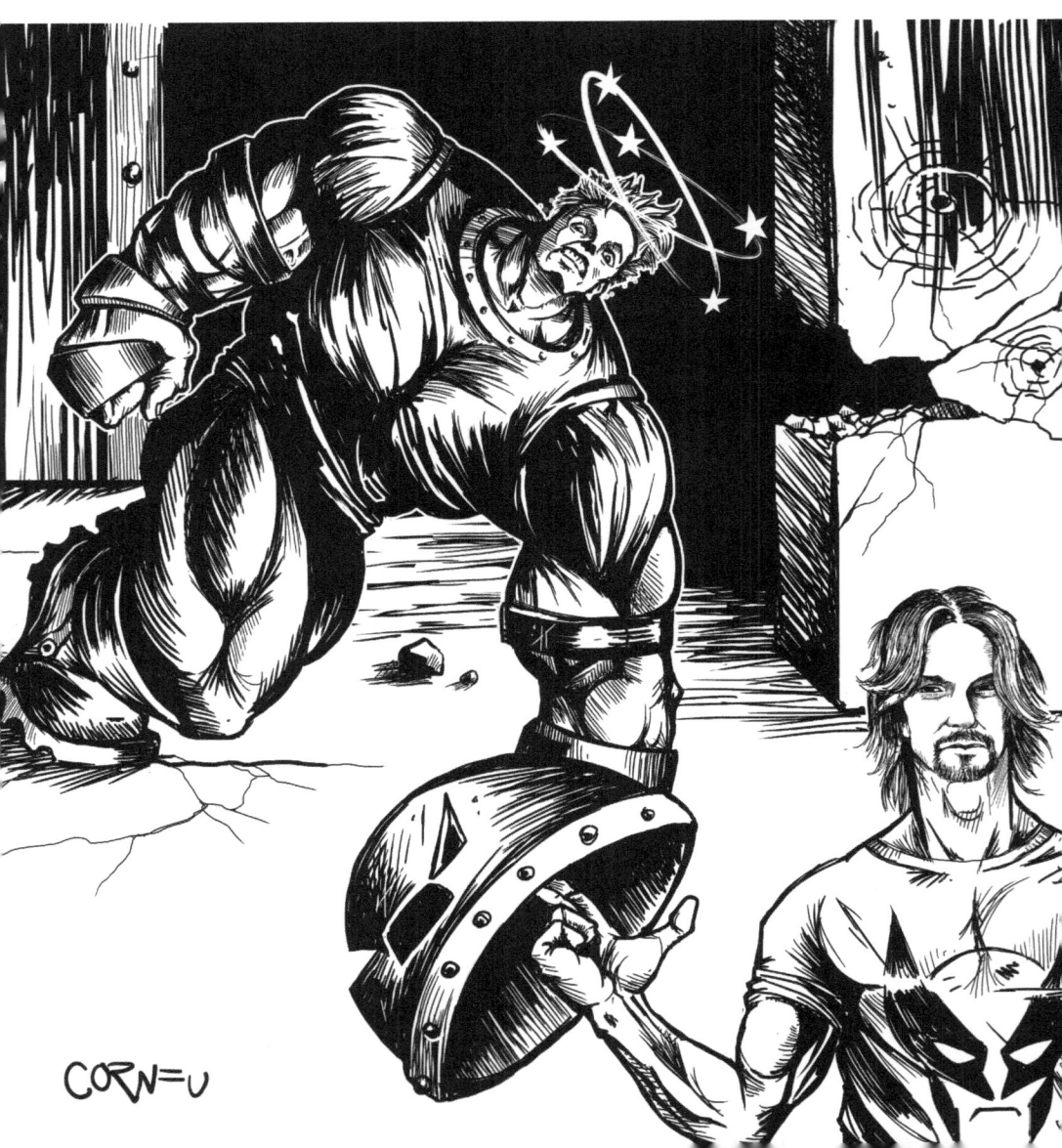

04 **CHALLENGE WORD:**
destroyer

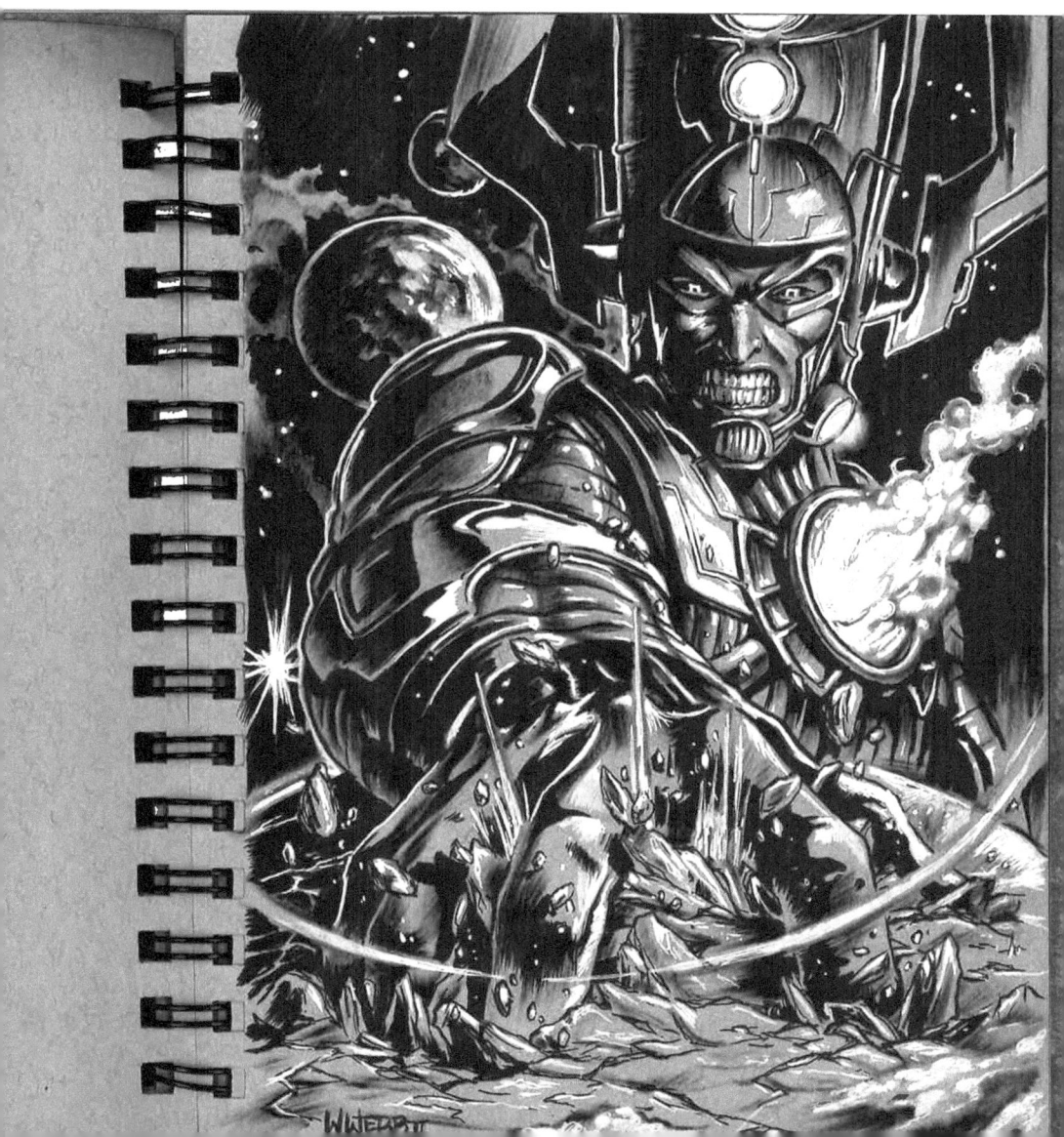

05 CHALLENGE WORD:
cryptic

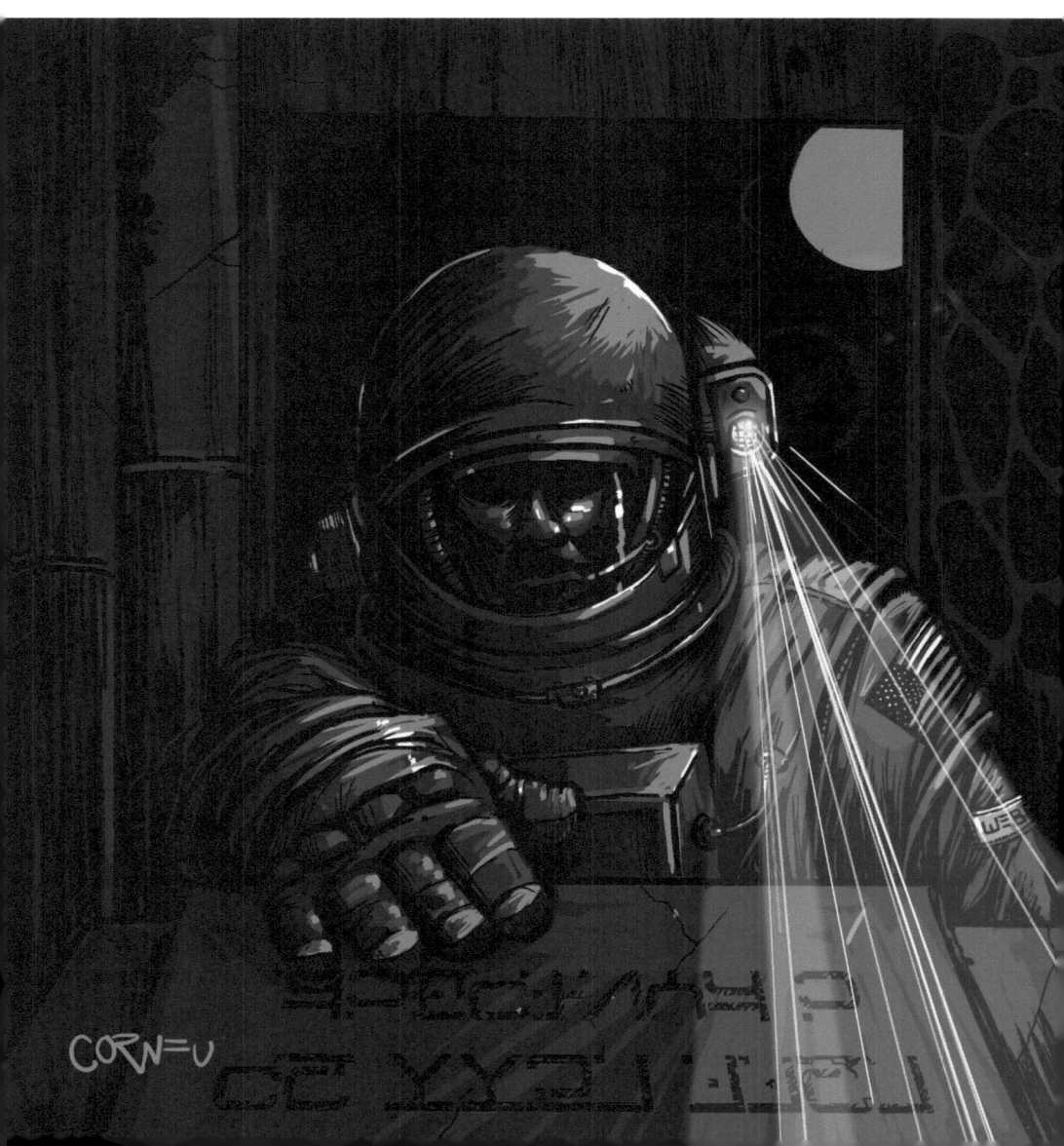

05 CHALLENGE WORD:
whiplash

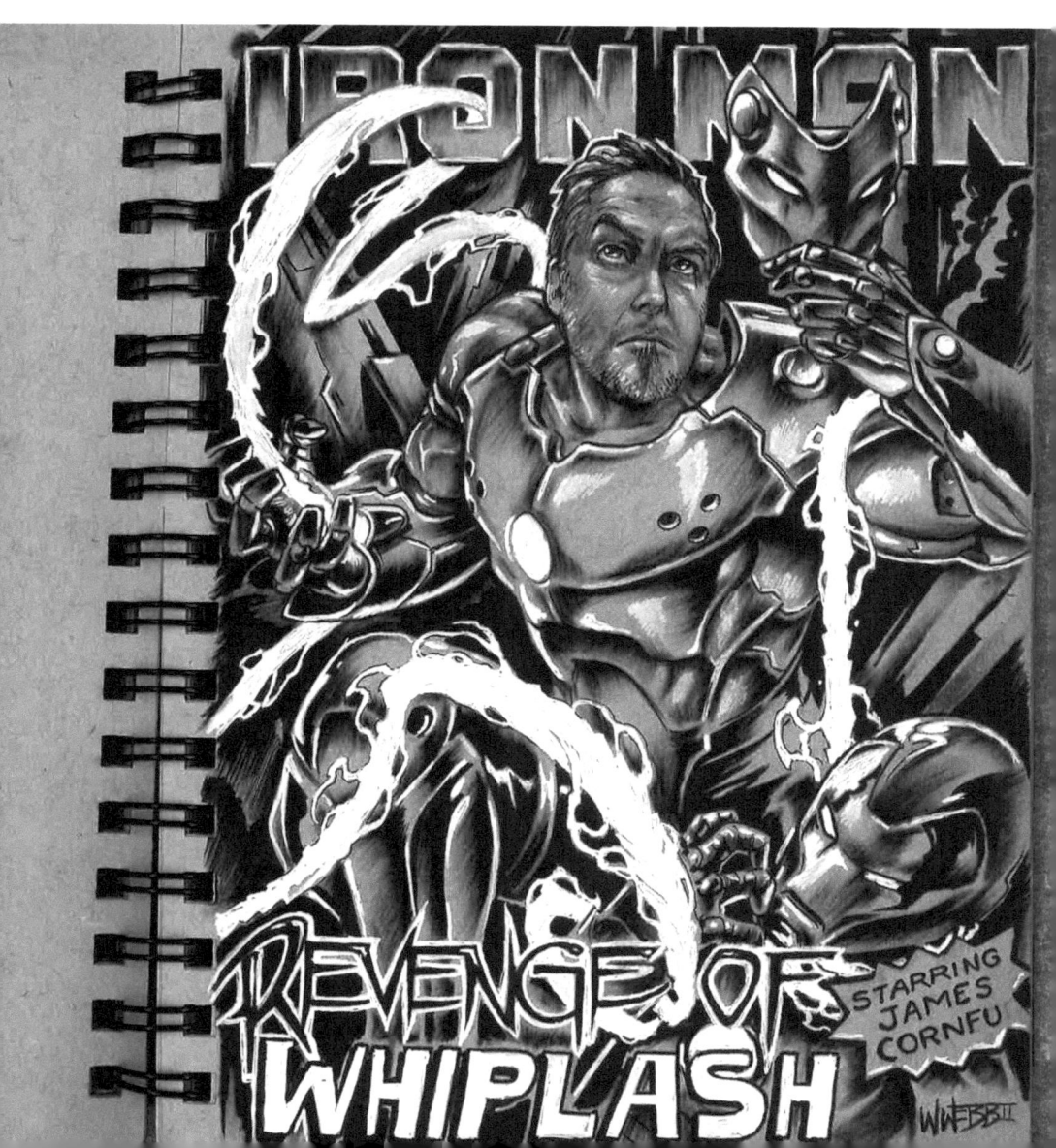

06 CHALLENGE WORD:
malediction

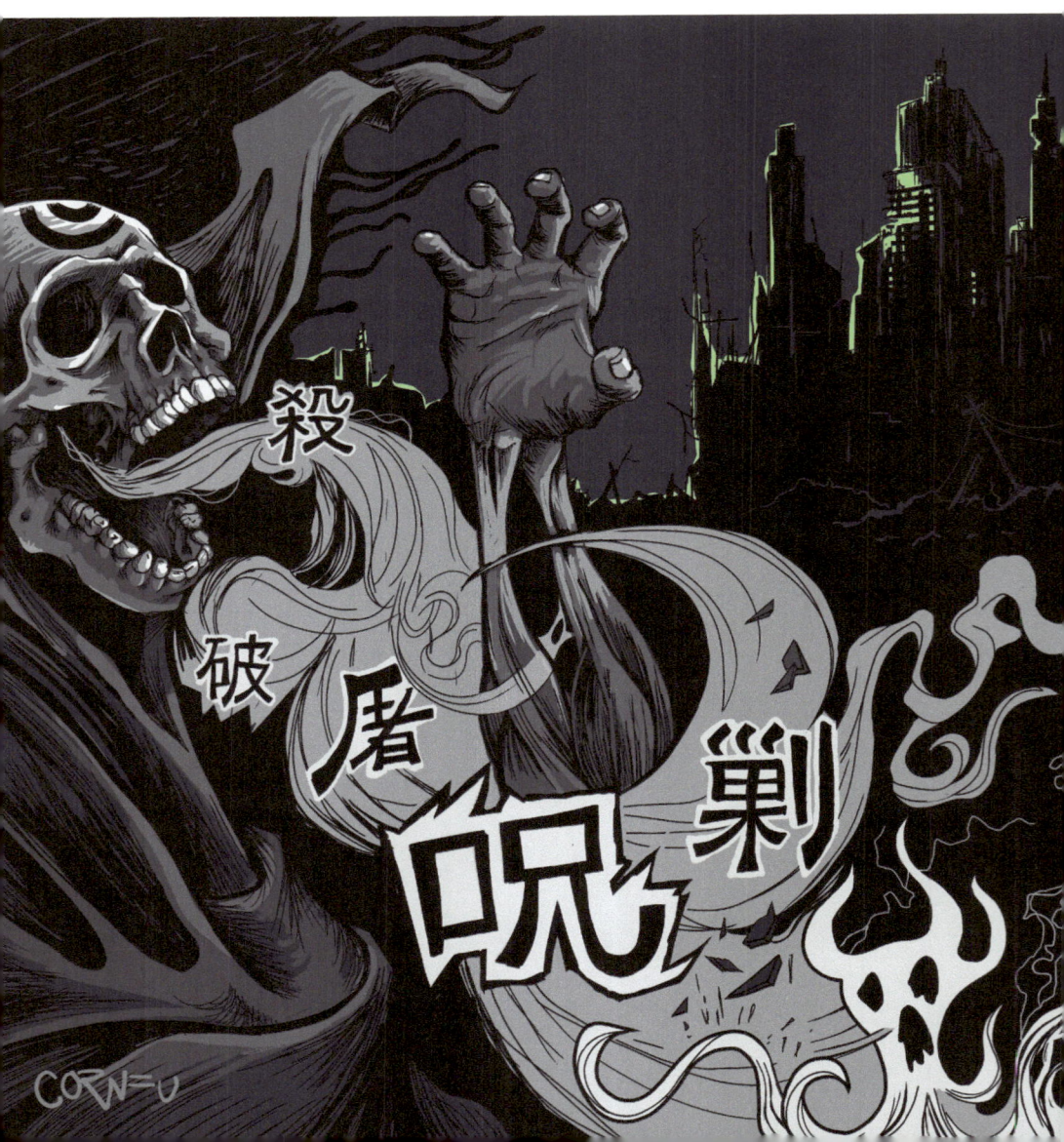

06 CHALLENGE WORD:
vengeance

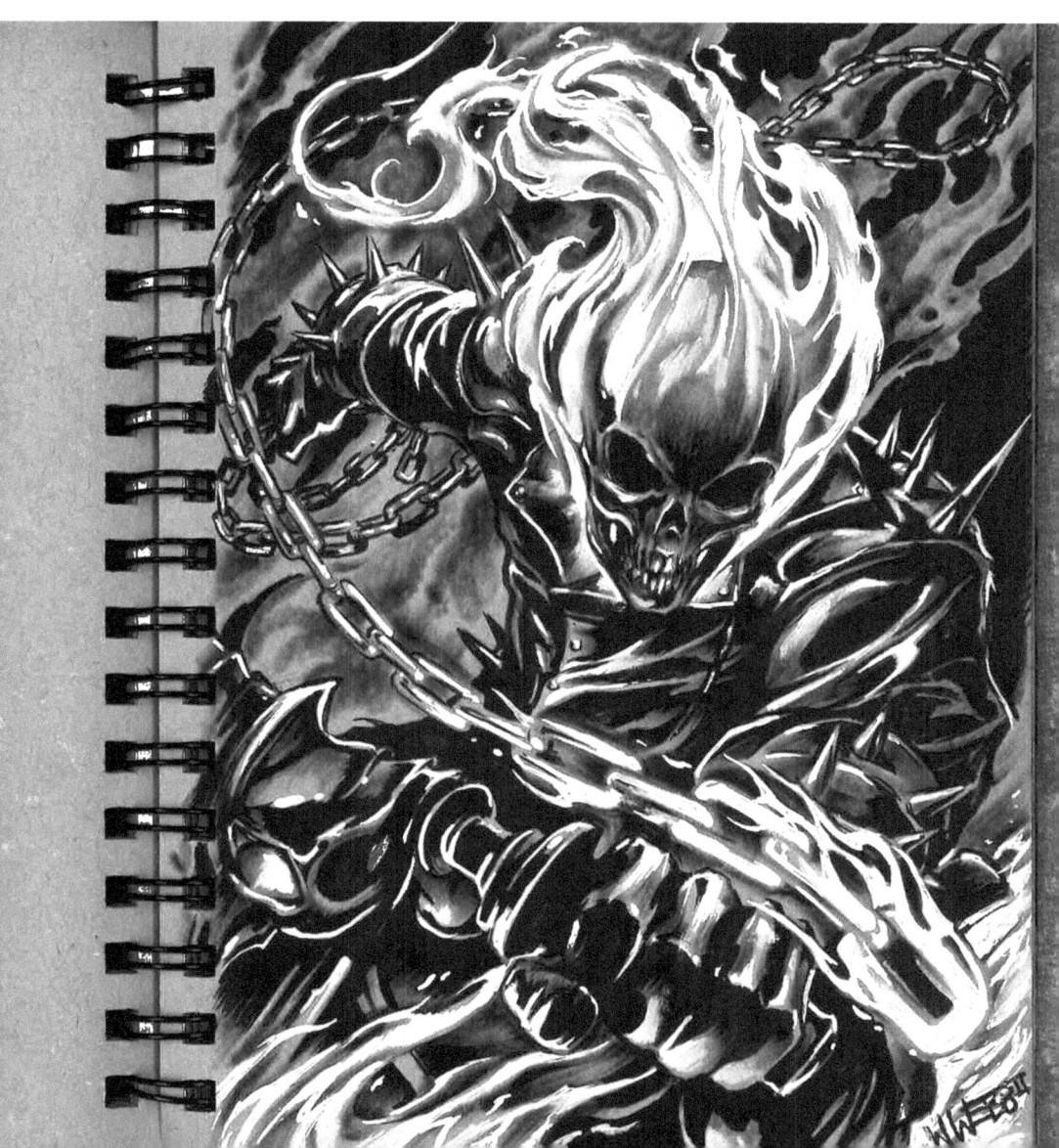

07 CHALLENGE WORD:
paladin

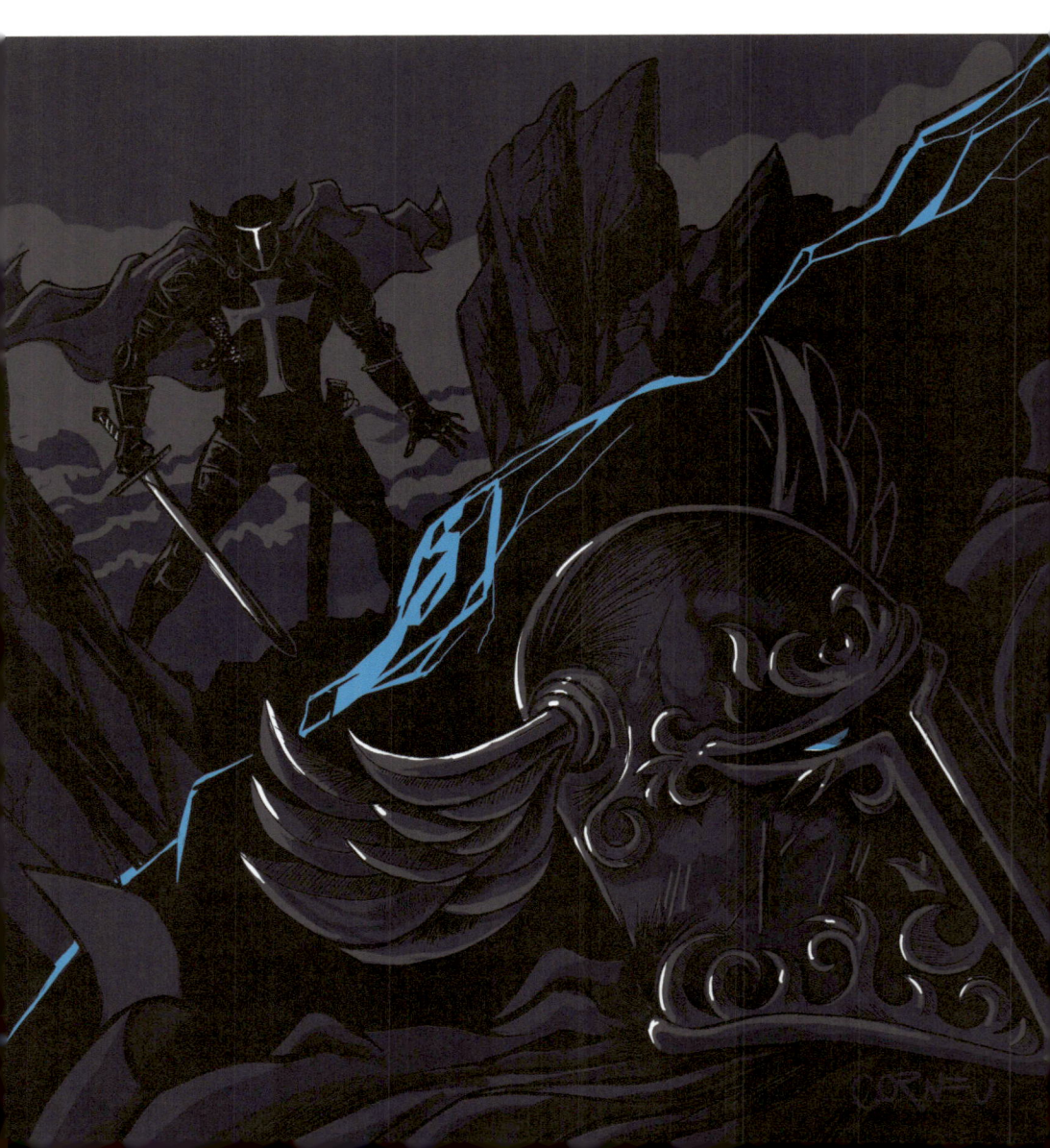

07 CHALLENGE WORD:
abaddon

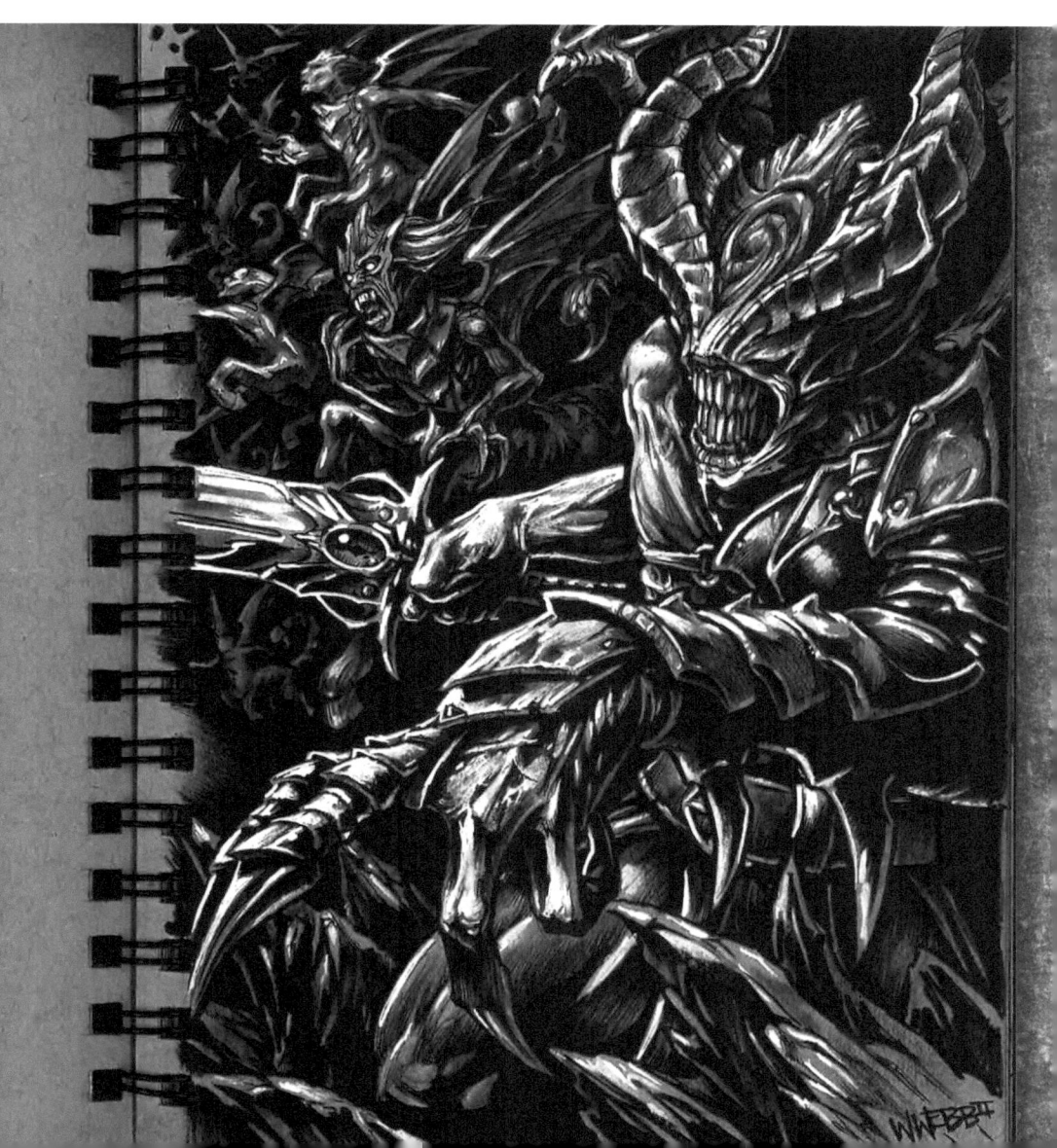

08 CHALLENGE WORD:
carnival

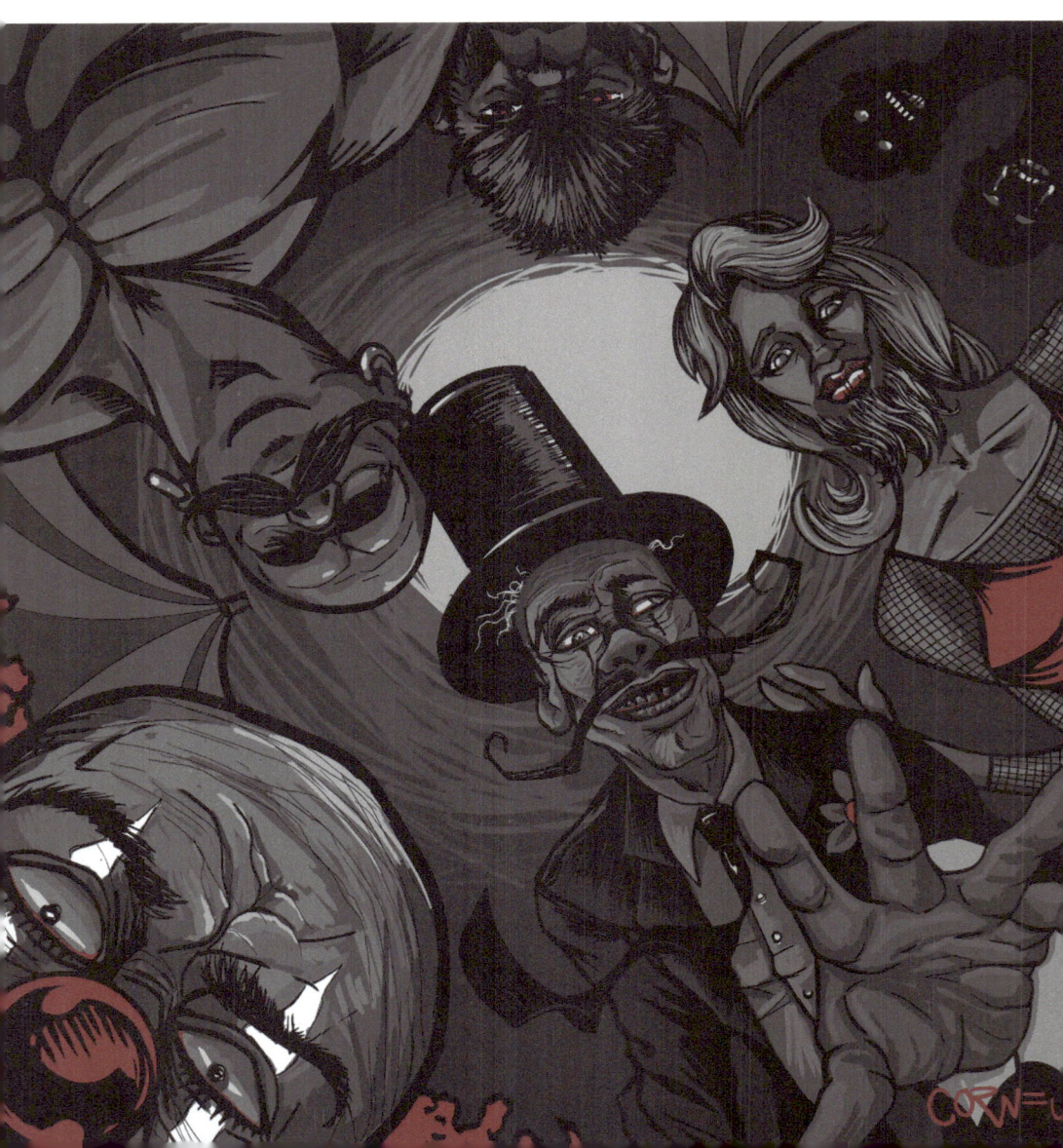

08 CHALLENGE WORD:
rabbit samurai

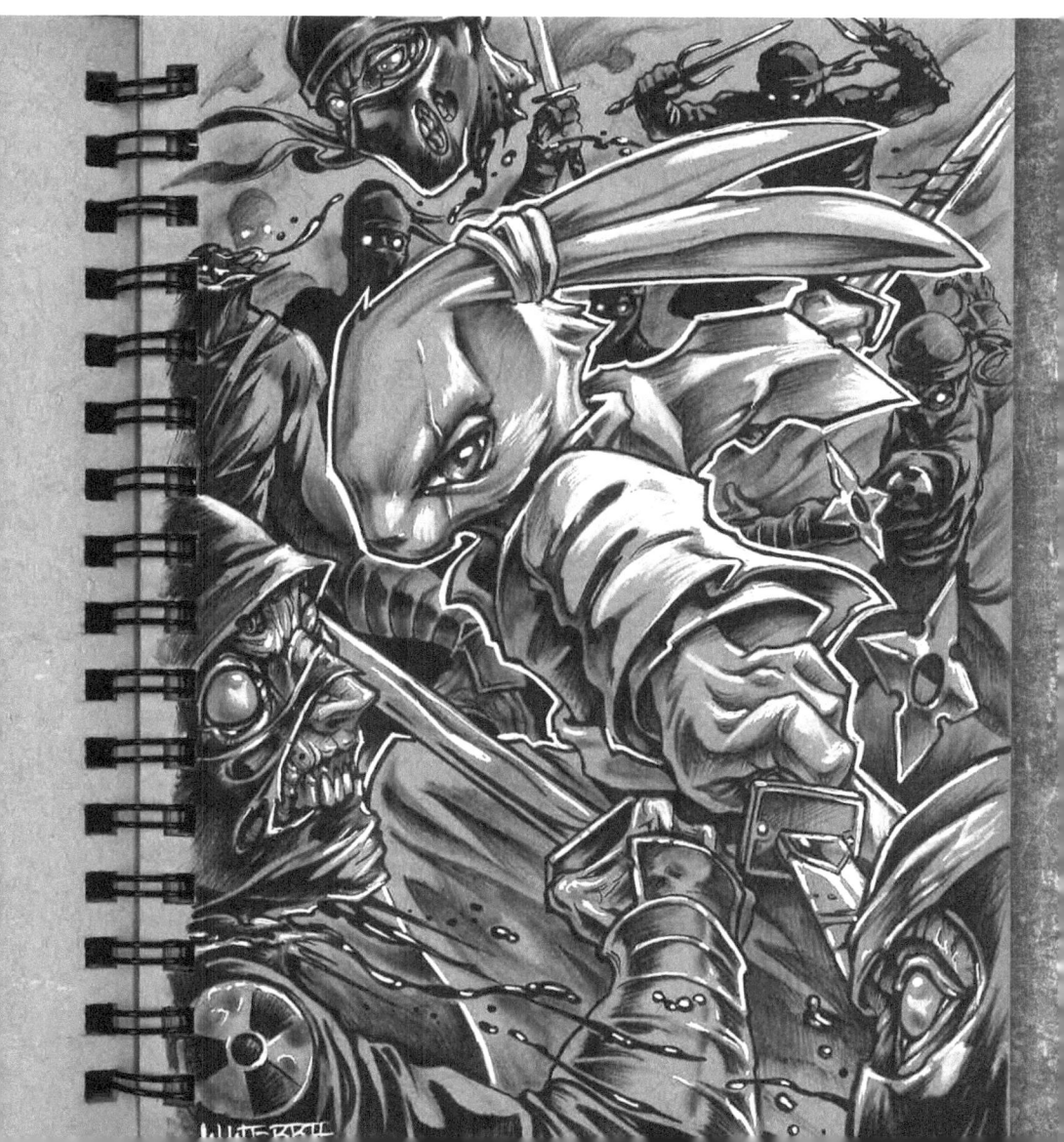

09 CHALLENGE WORD:
morning star

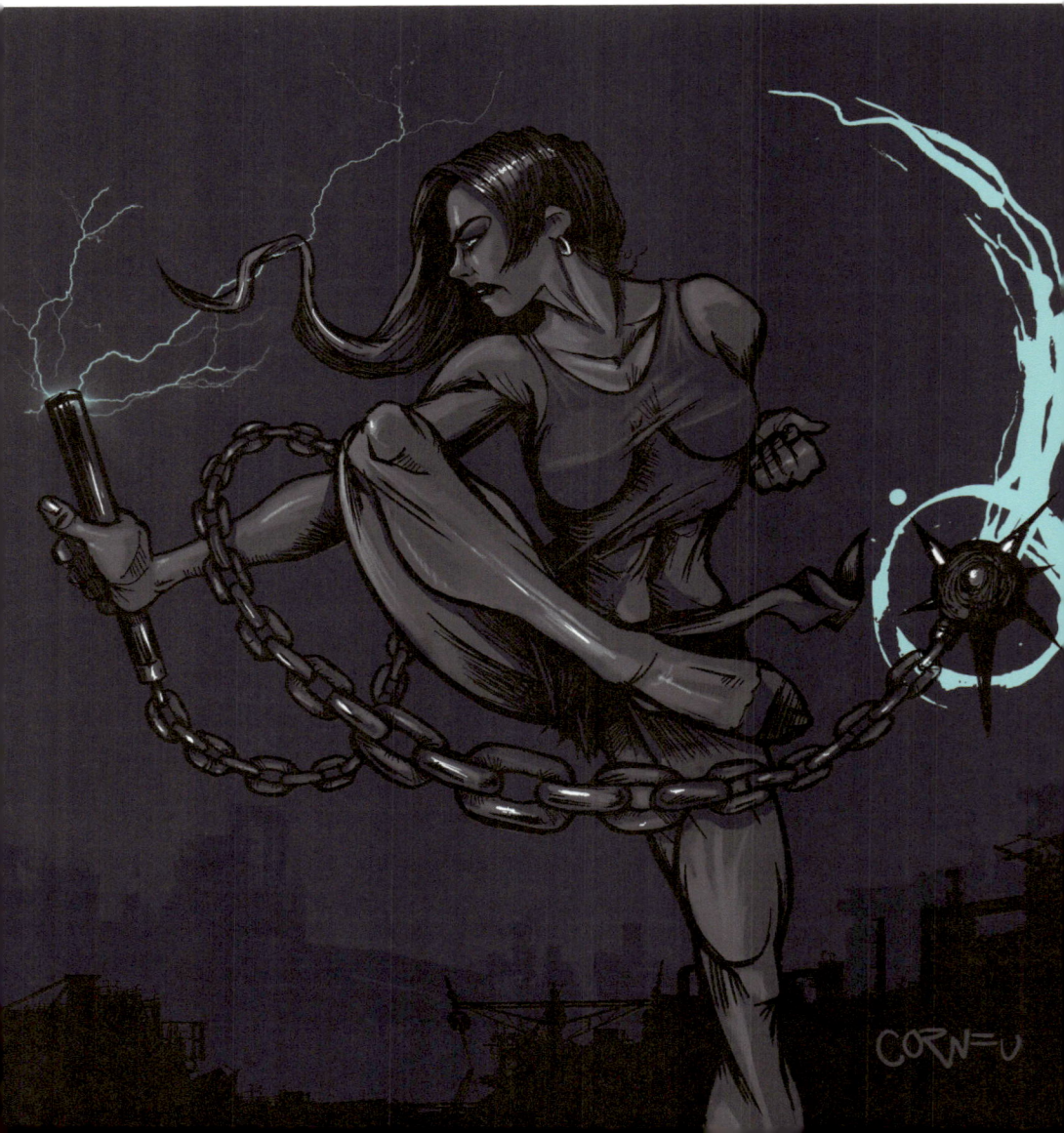

09 CHALLENGE WORD:
pack

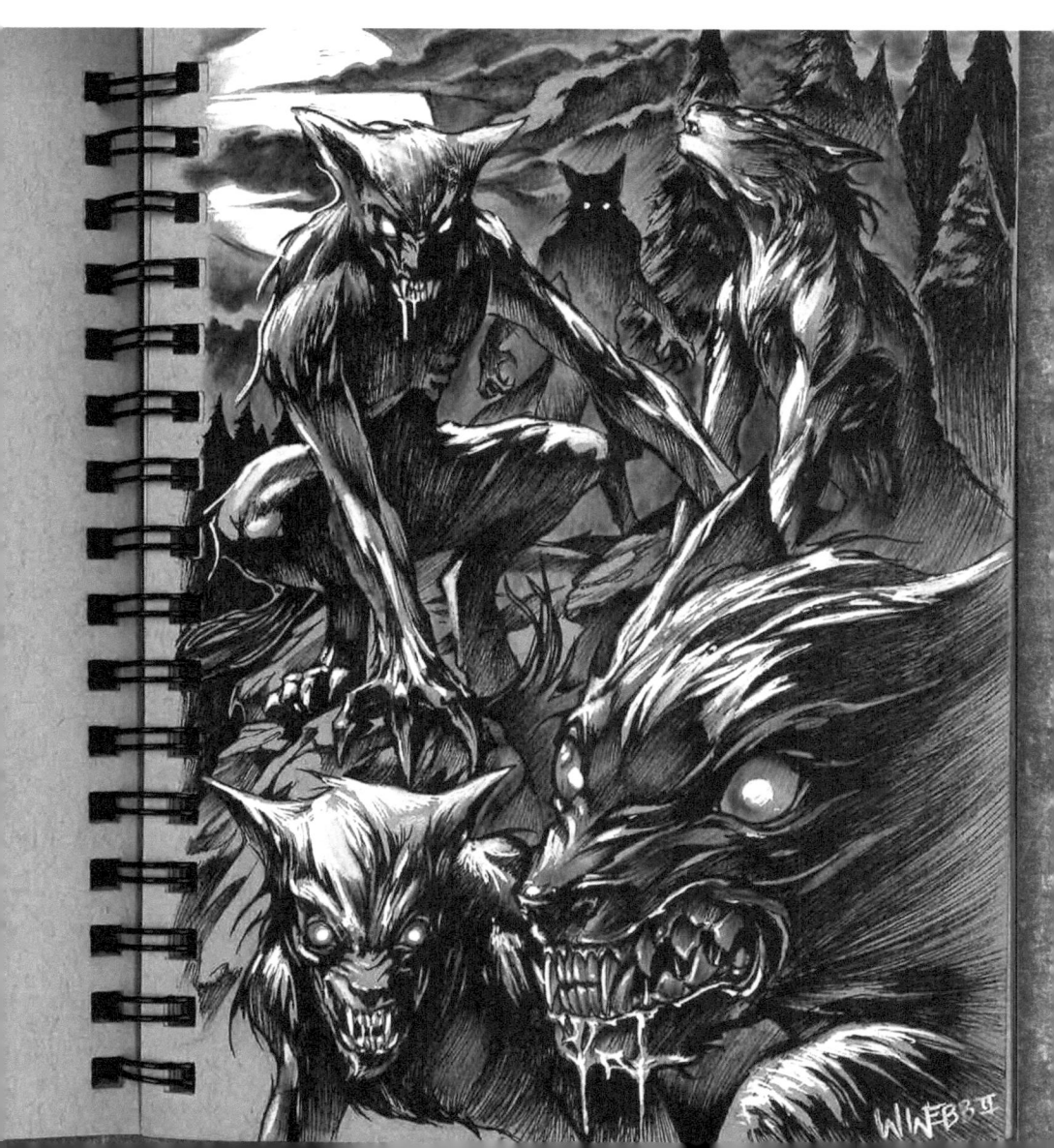

10 CHALLENGE WORD:
speed

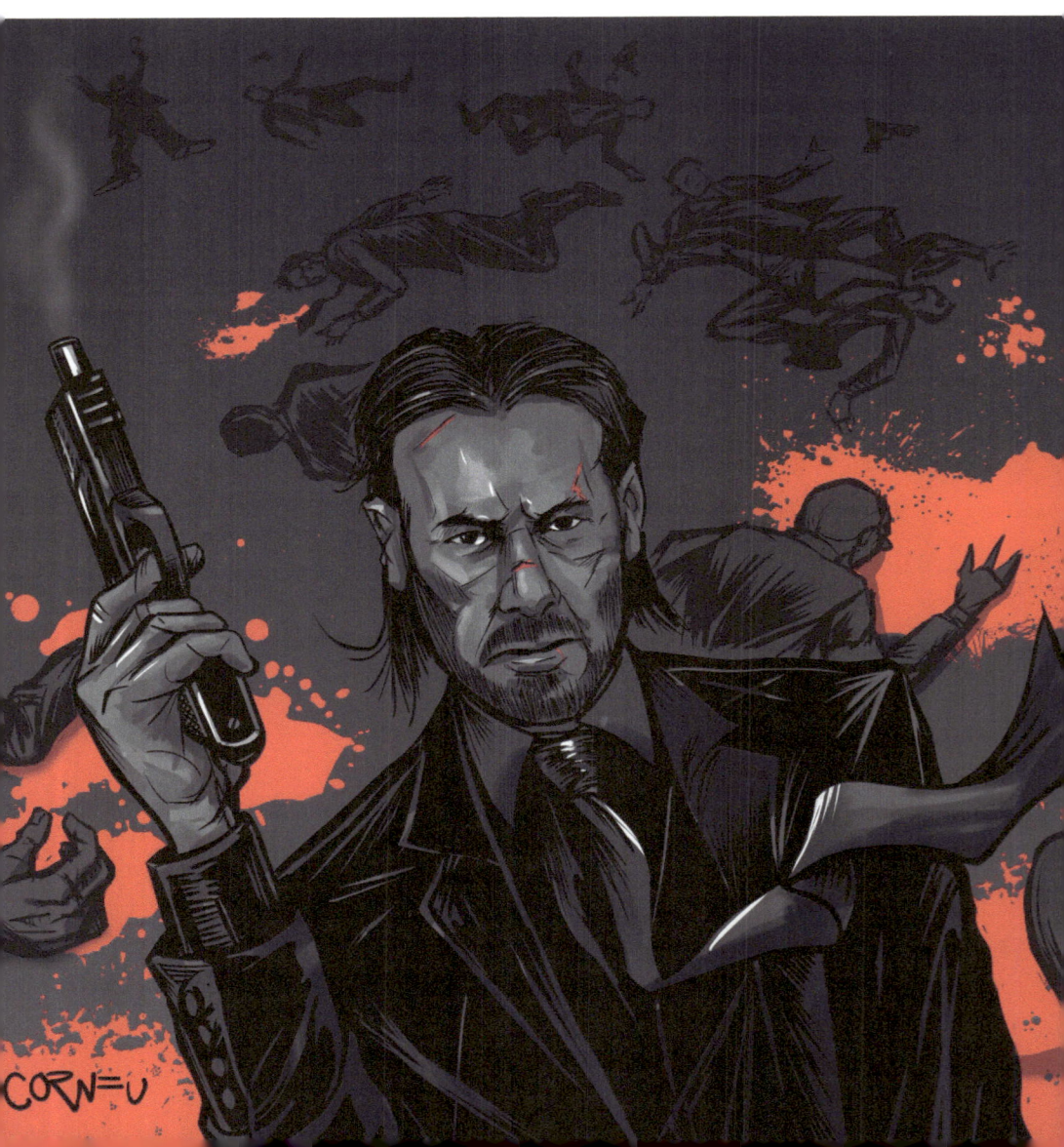

10 CHALLENGE WORD:
courage

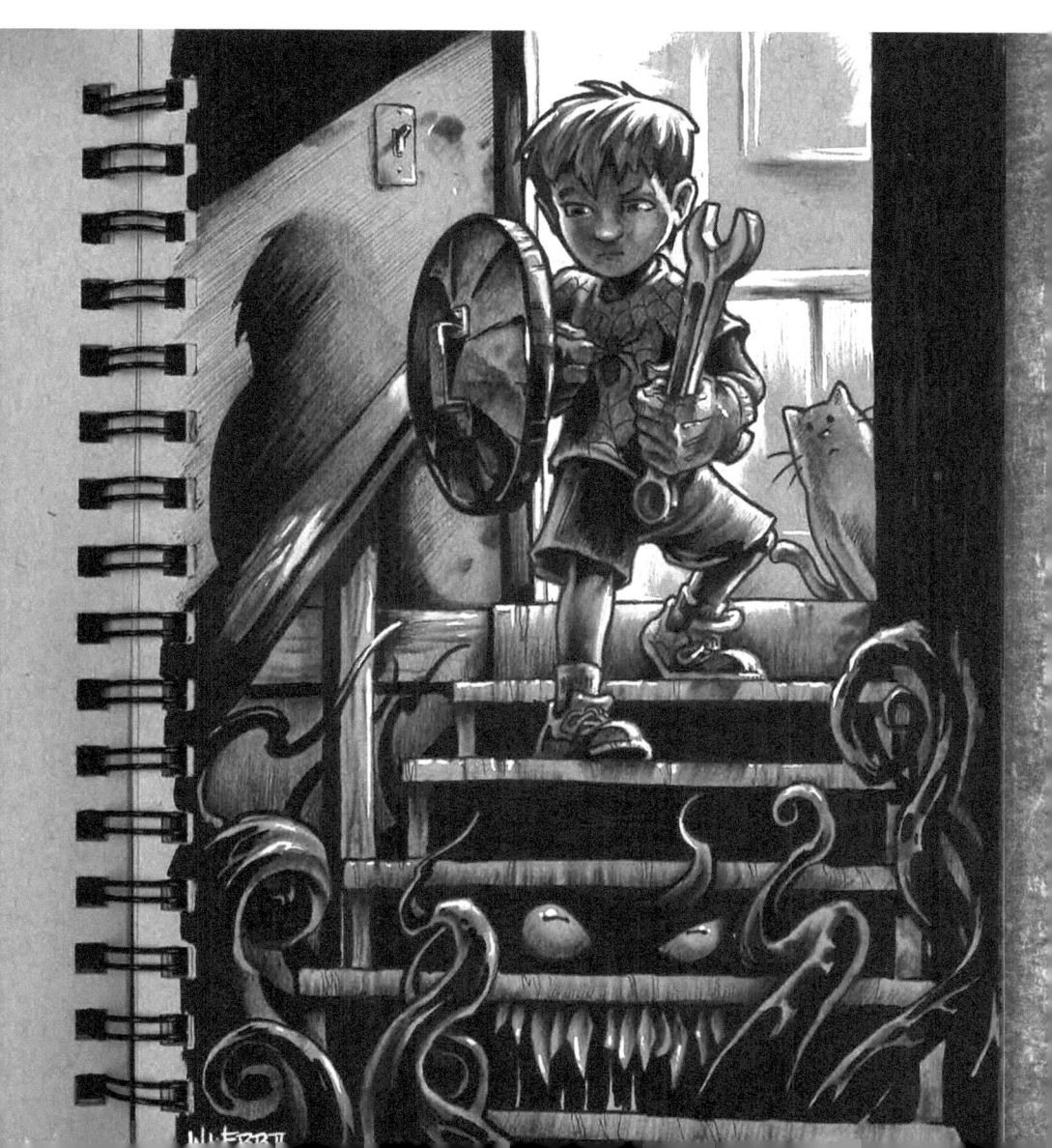

11 CHALLENGE WORD:
containment

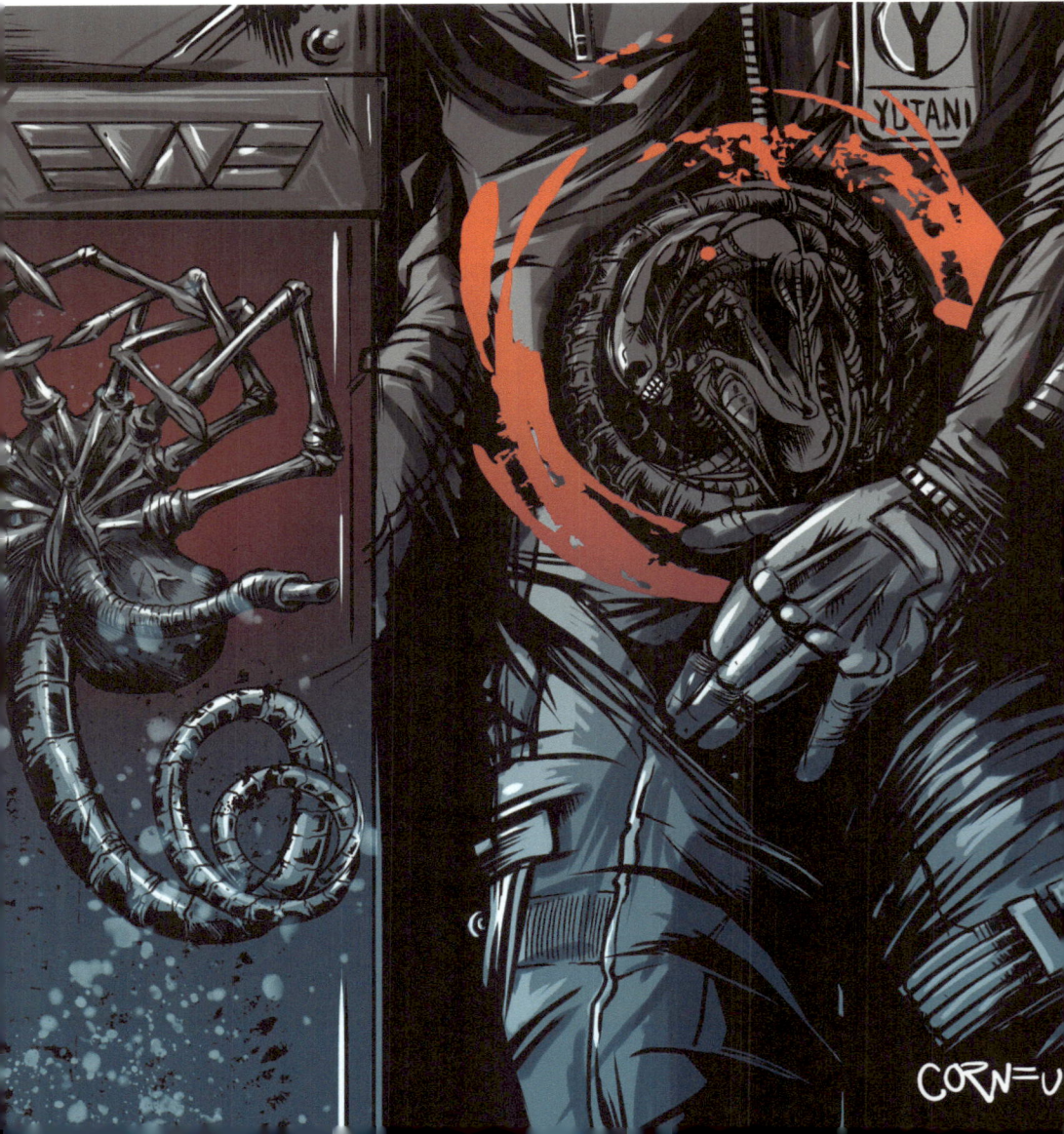

11 CHALLENGE WORD:
kamaitachi

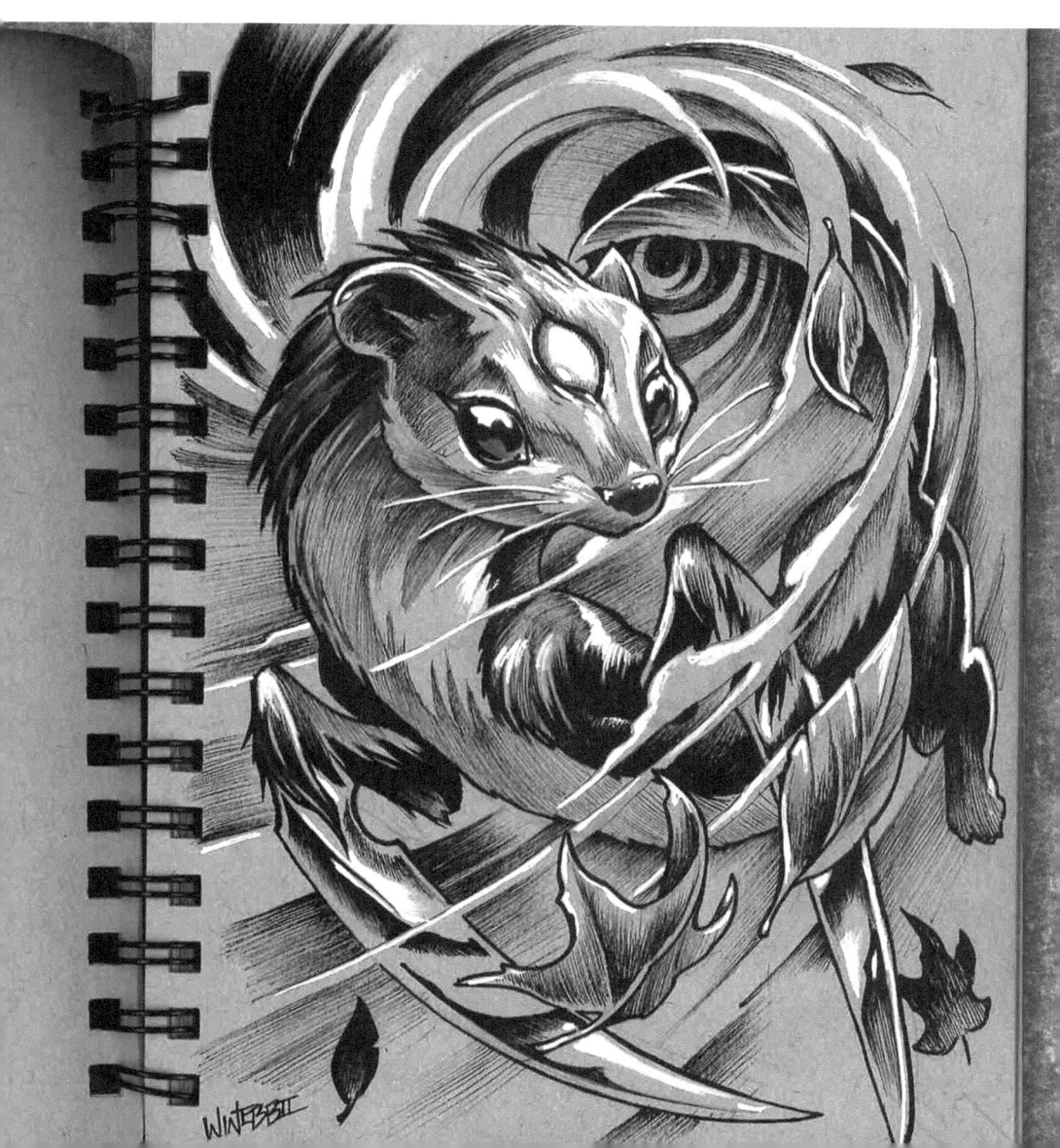

12 CHALLENGE WORD:
lunar

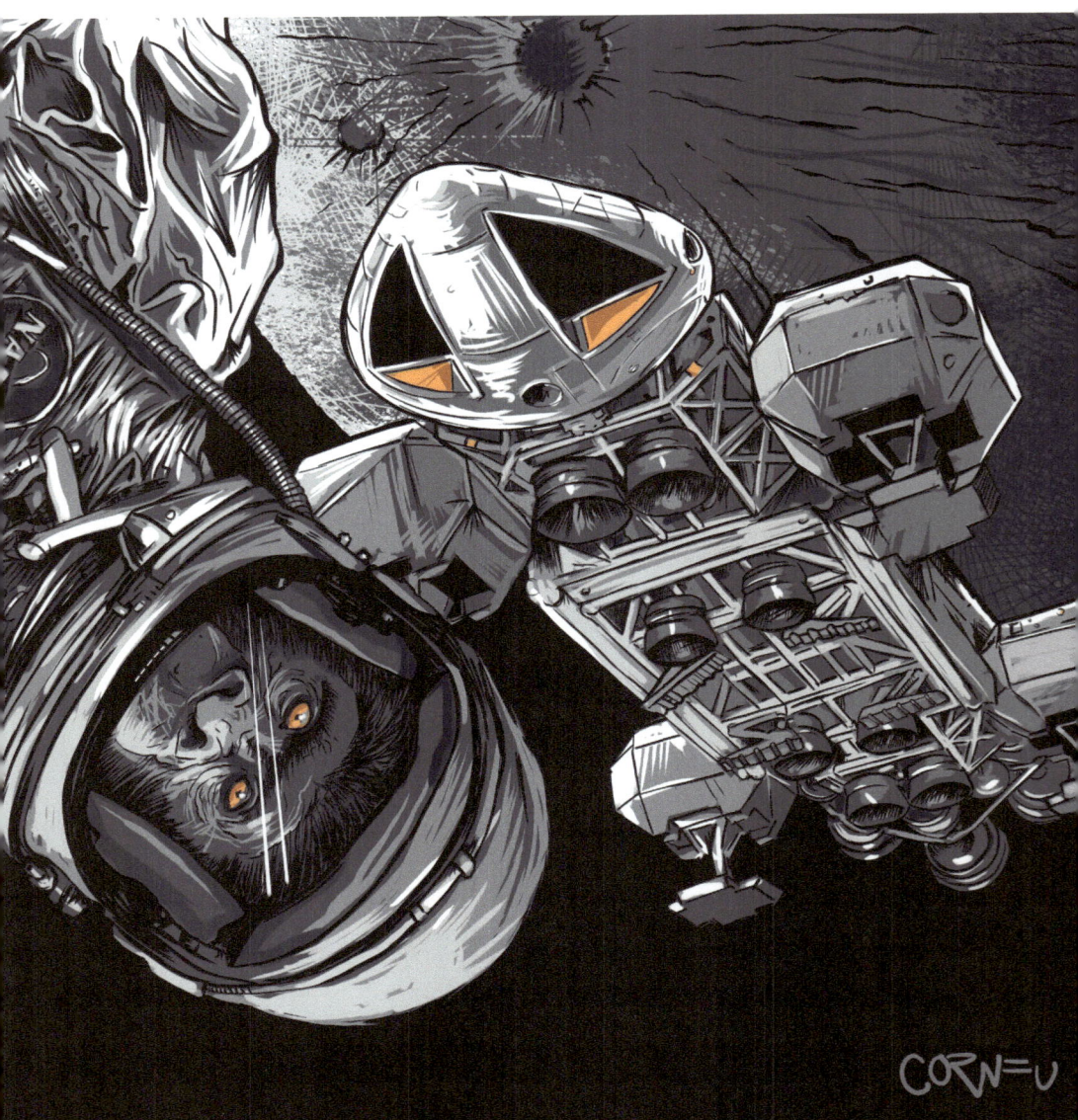

12 CHALLENGE WORD: robot

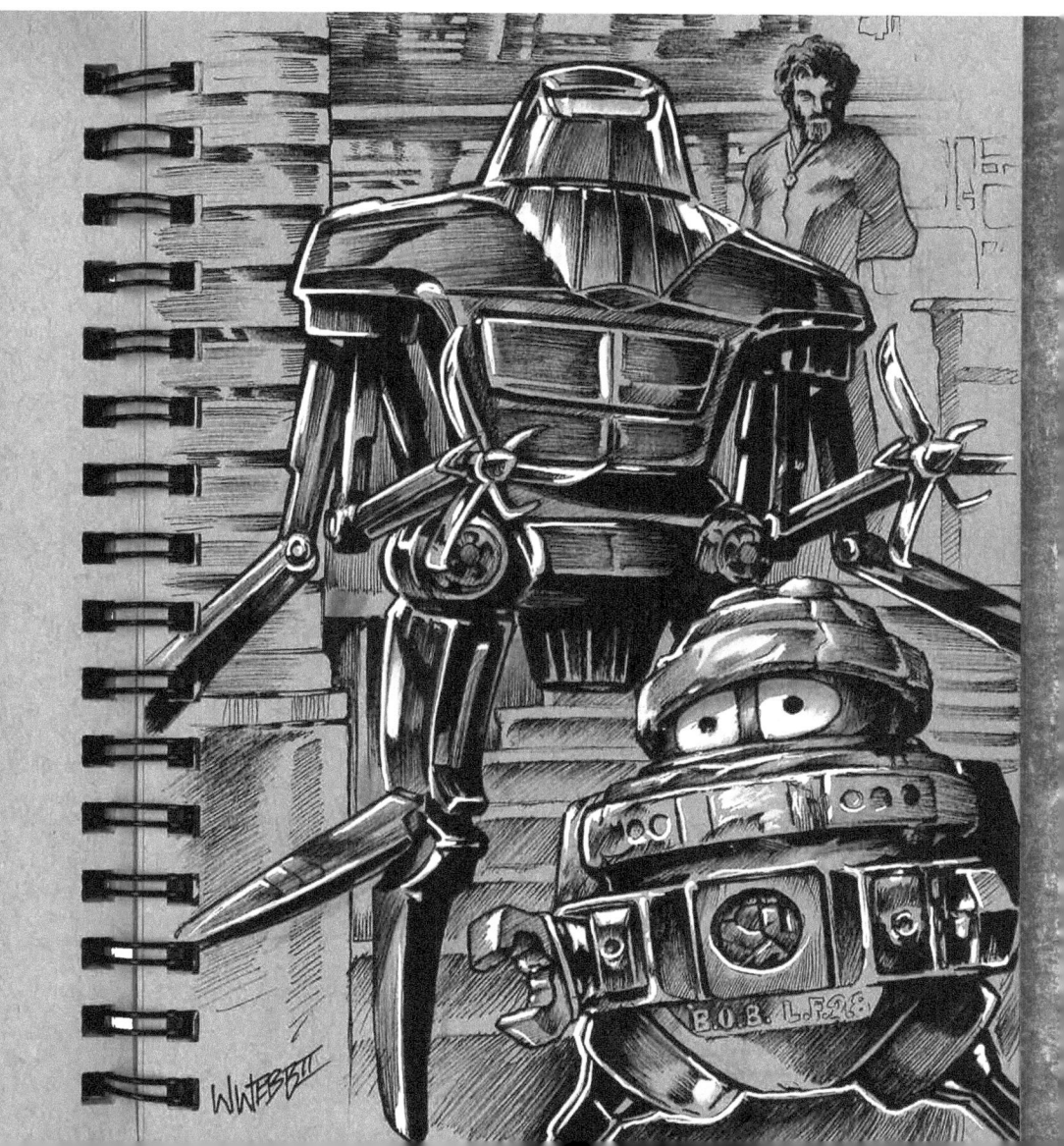

13 CHALLENGE WORD:
behemoth

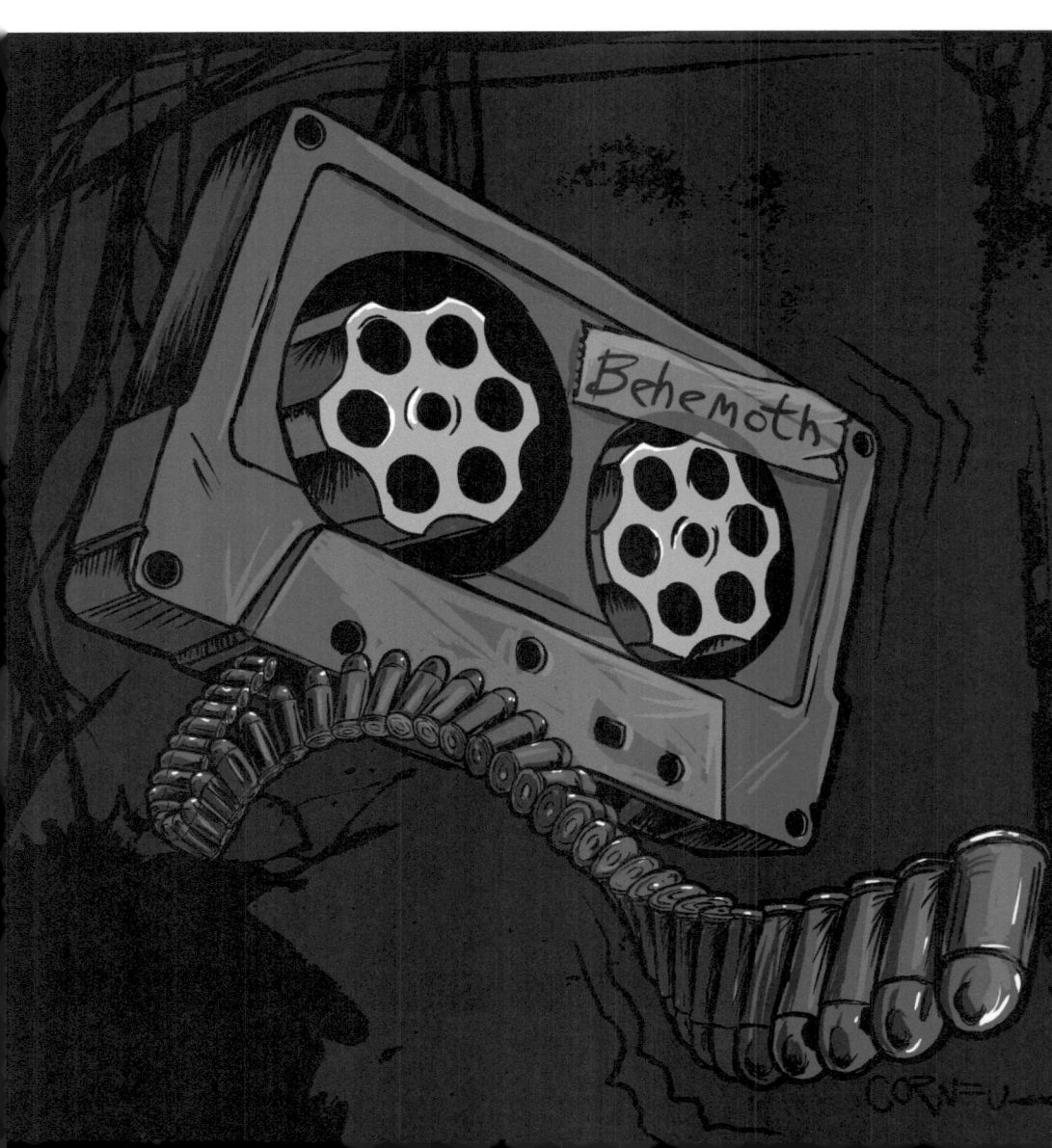

13 CHALLENGE WORD: bloat

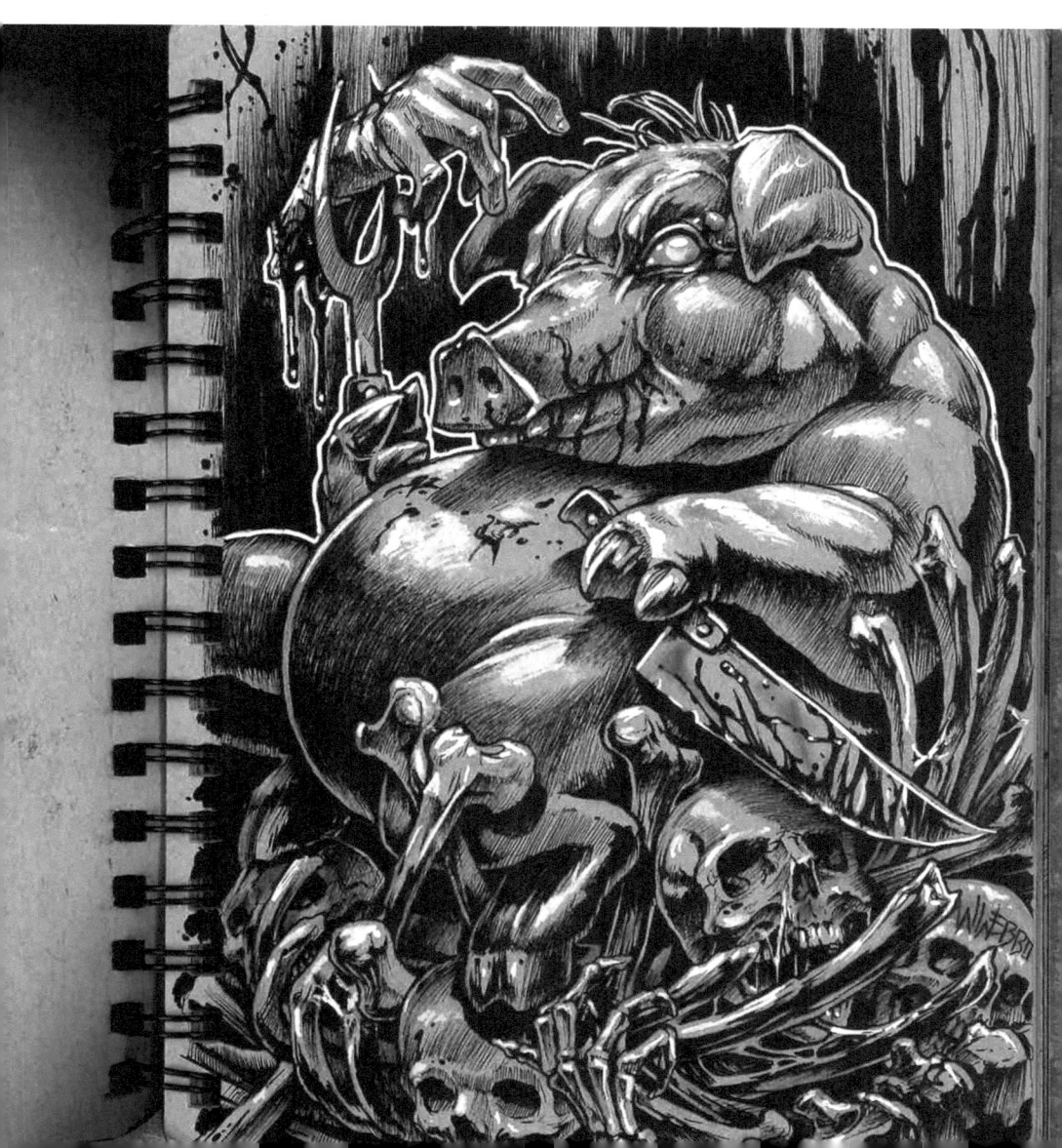

OVERACHIEVER MODE
bounty hunter (part 2)

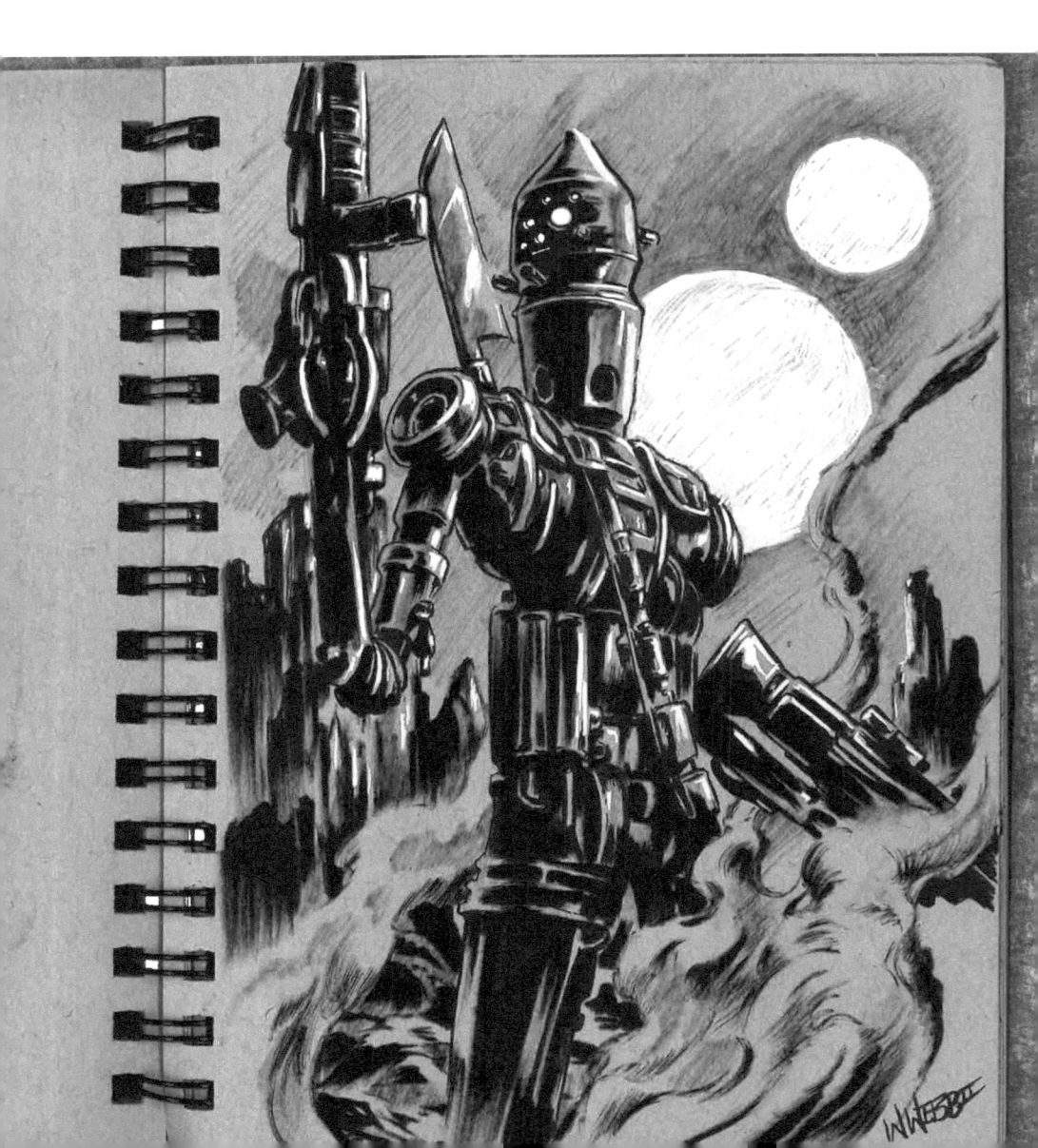

OVERACHIEVER MODE
destroyer (part 2)

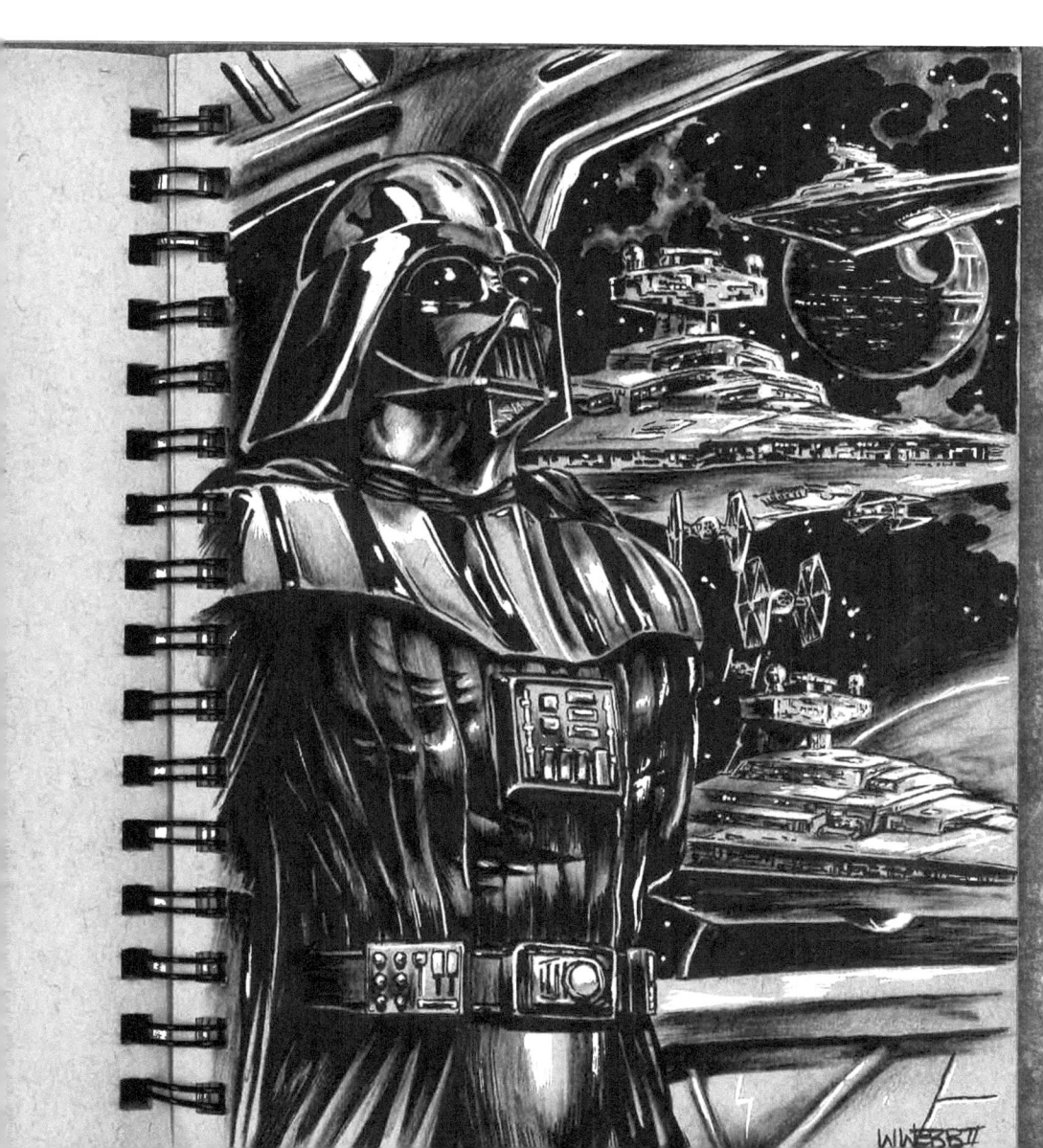

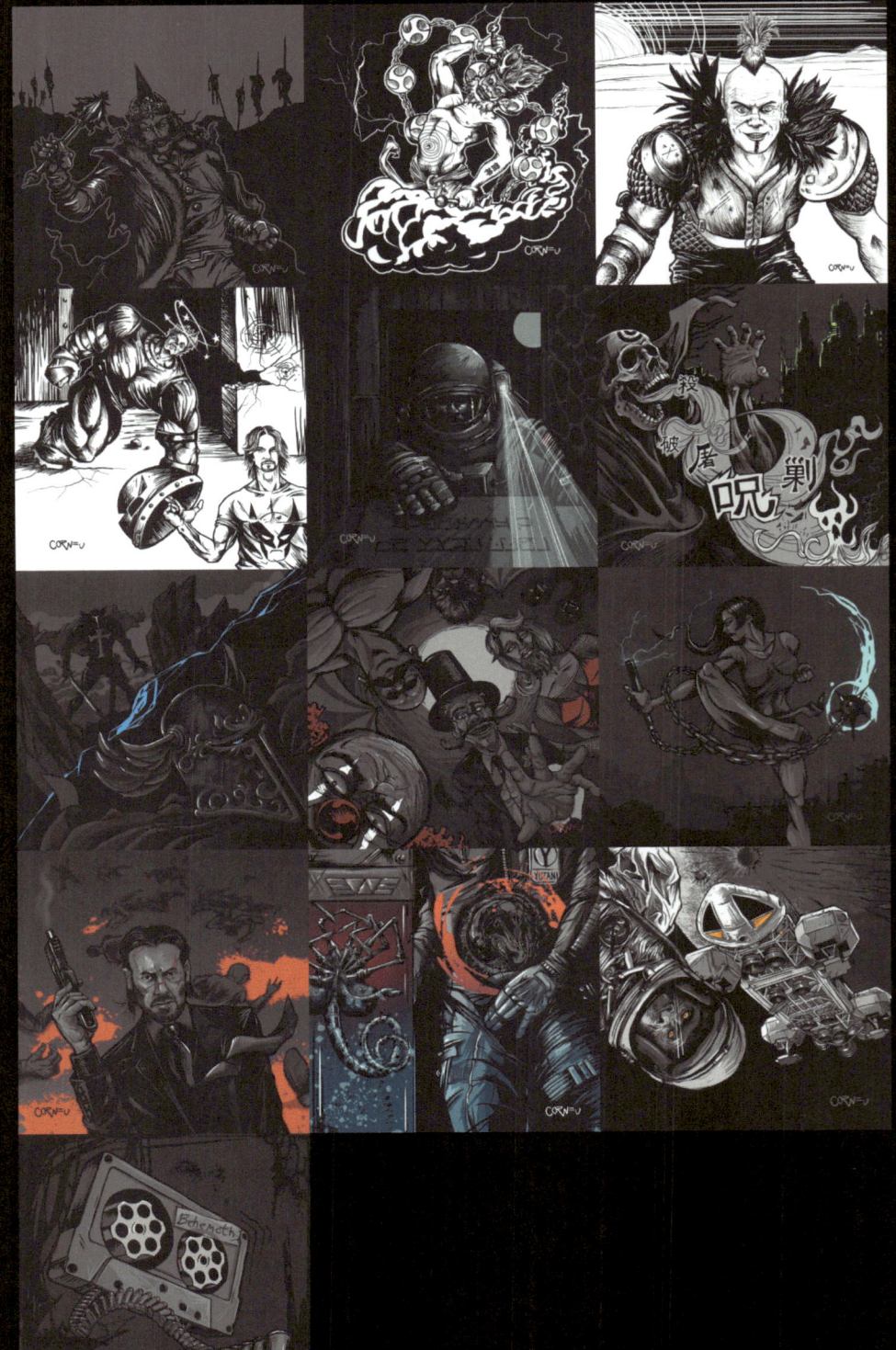

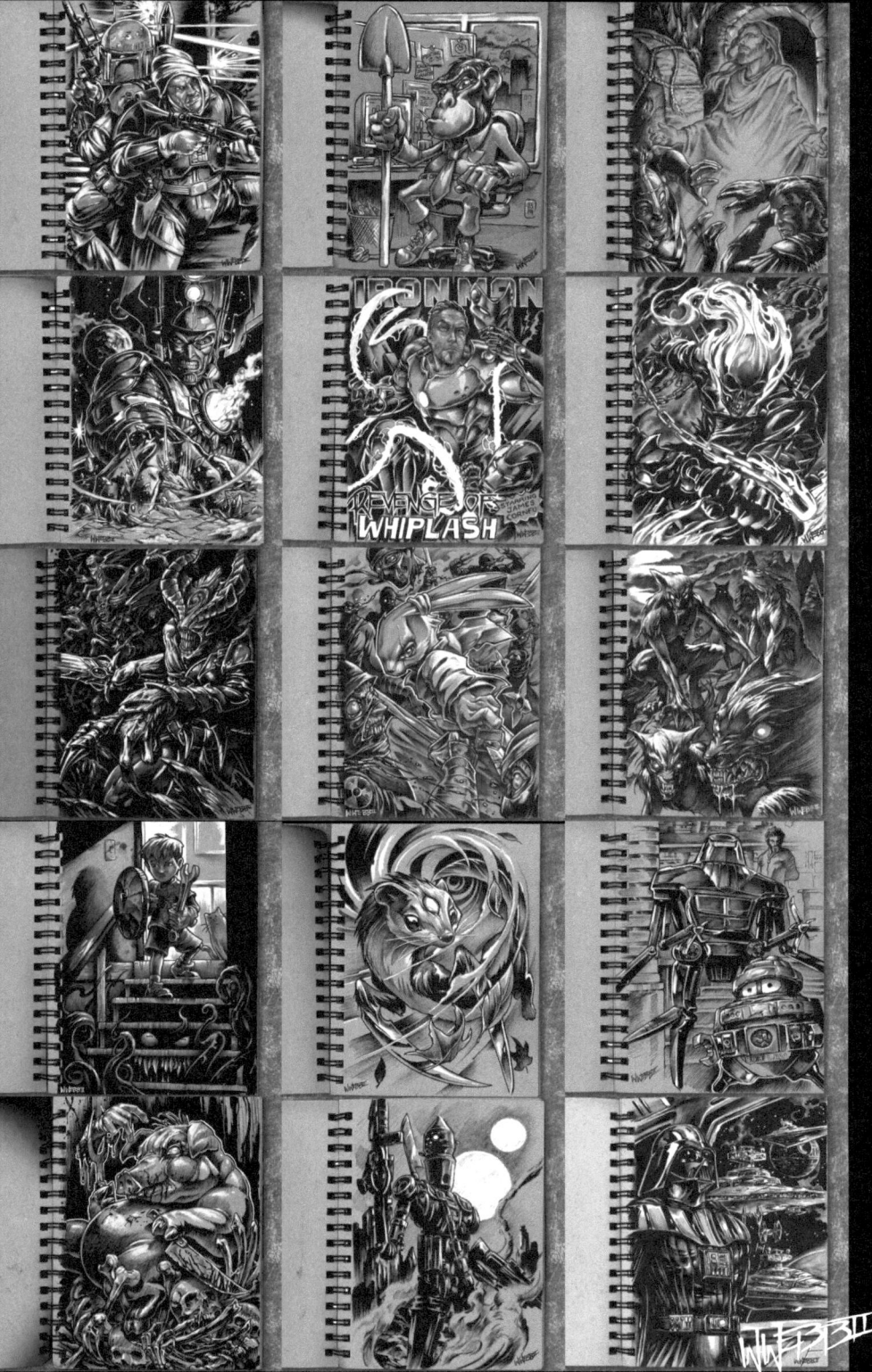

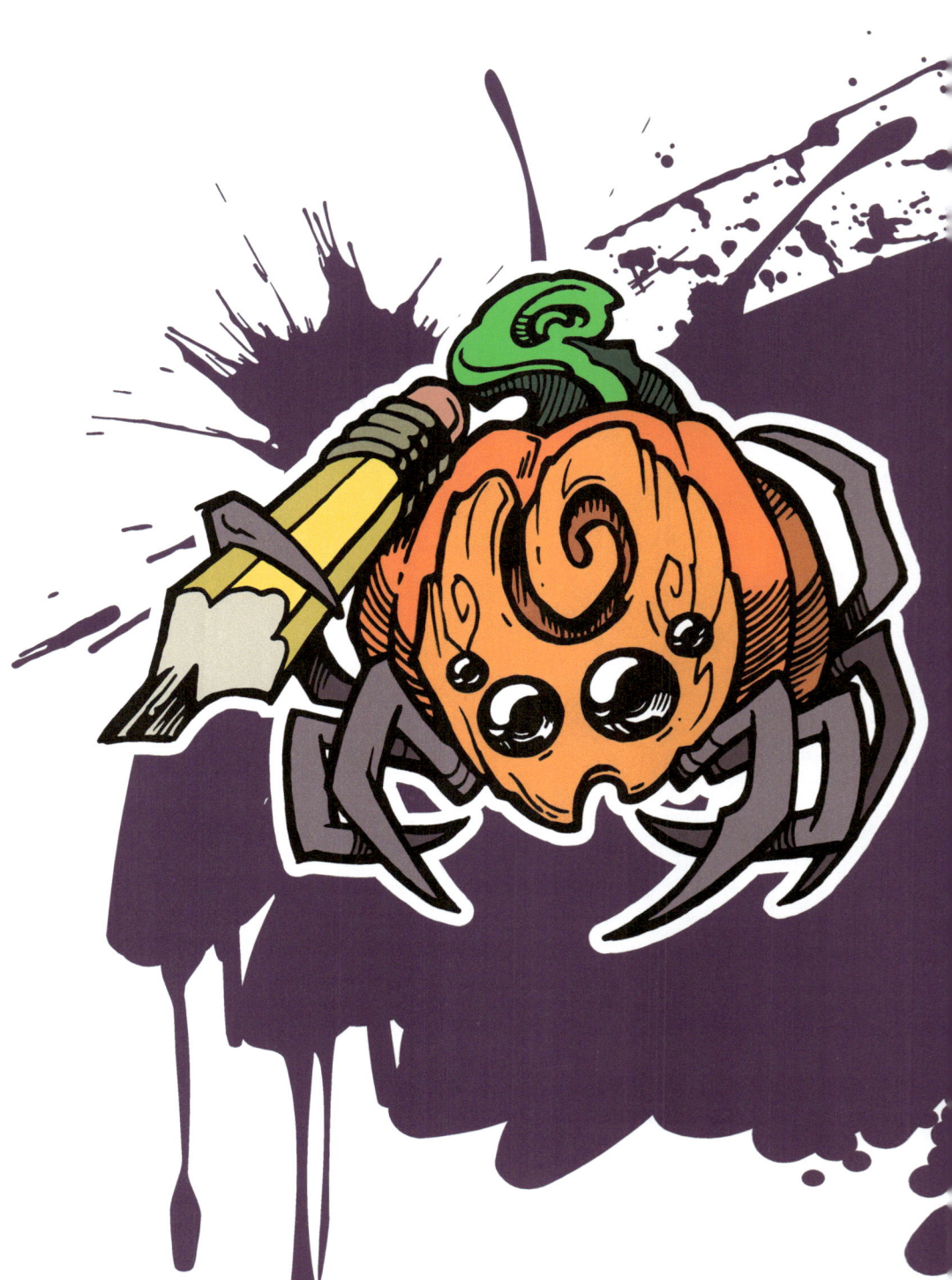

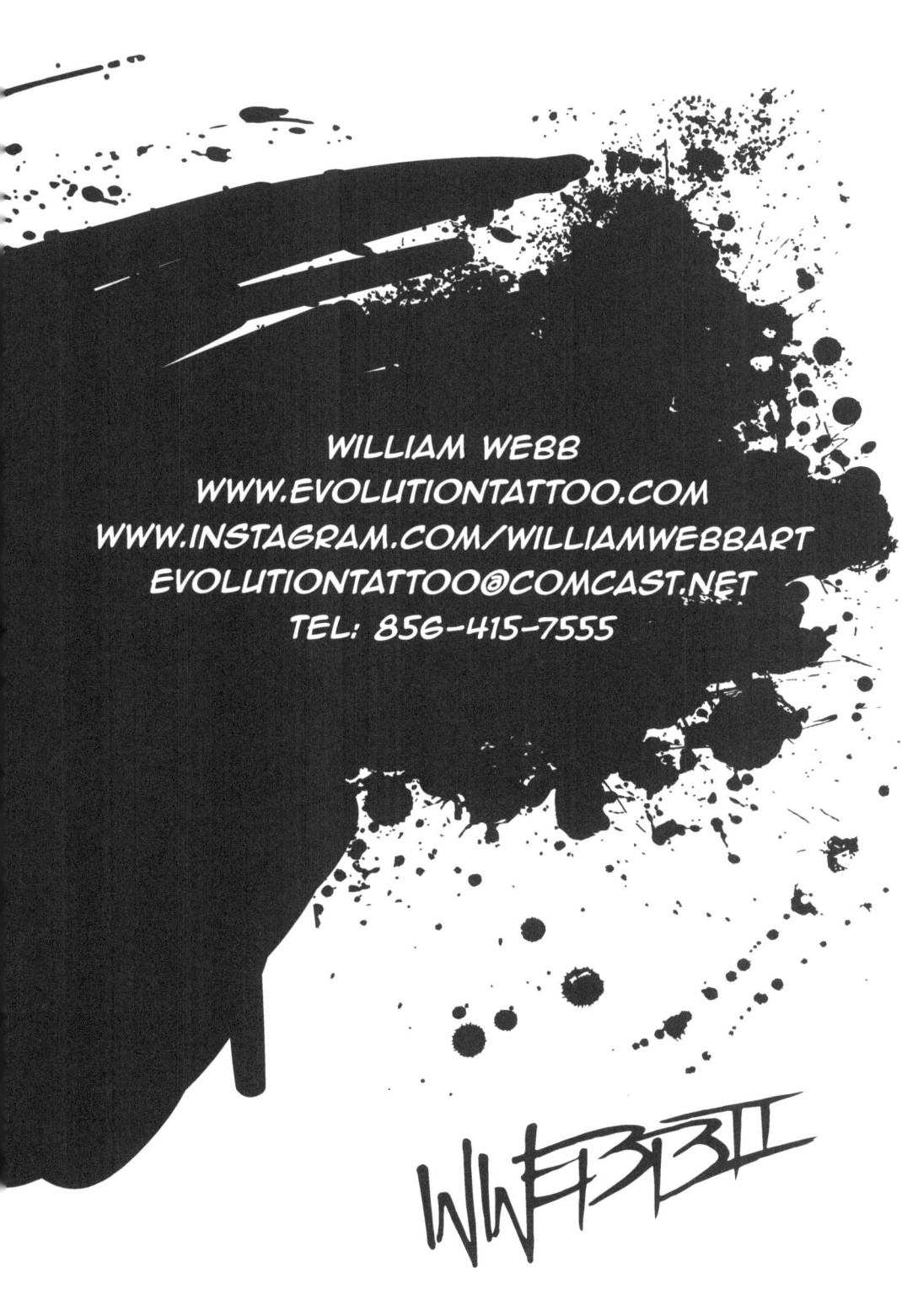

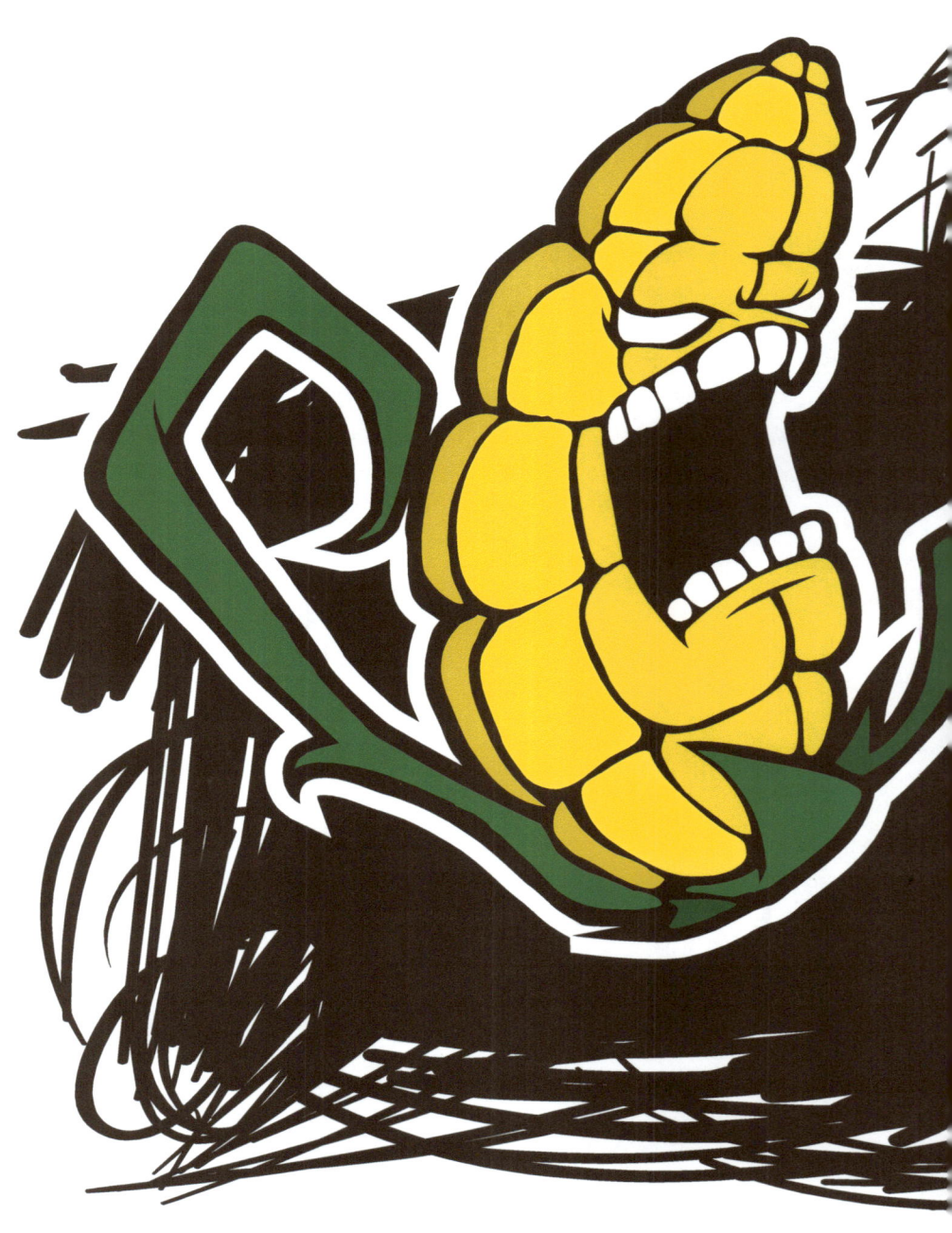

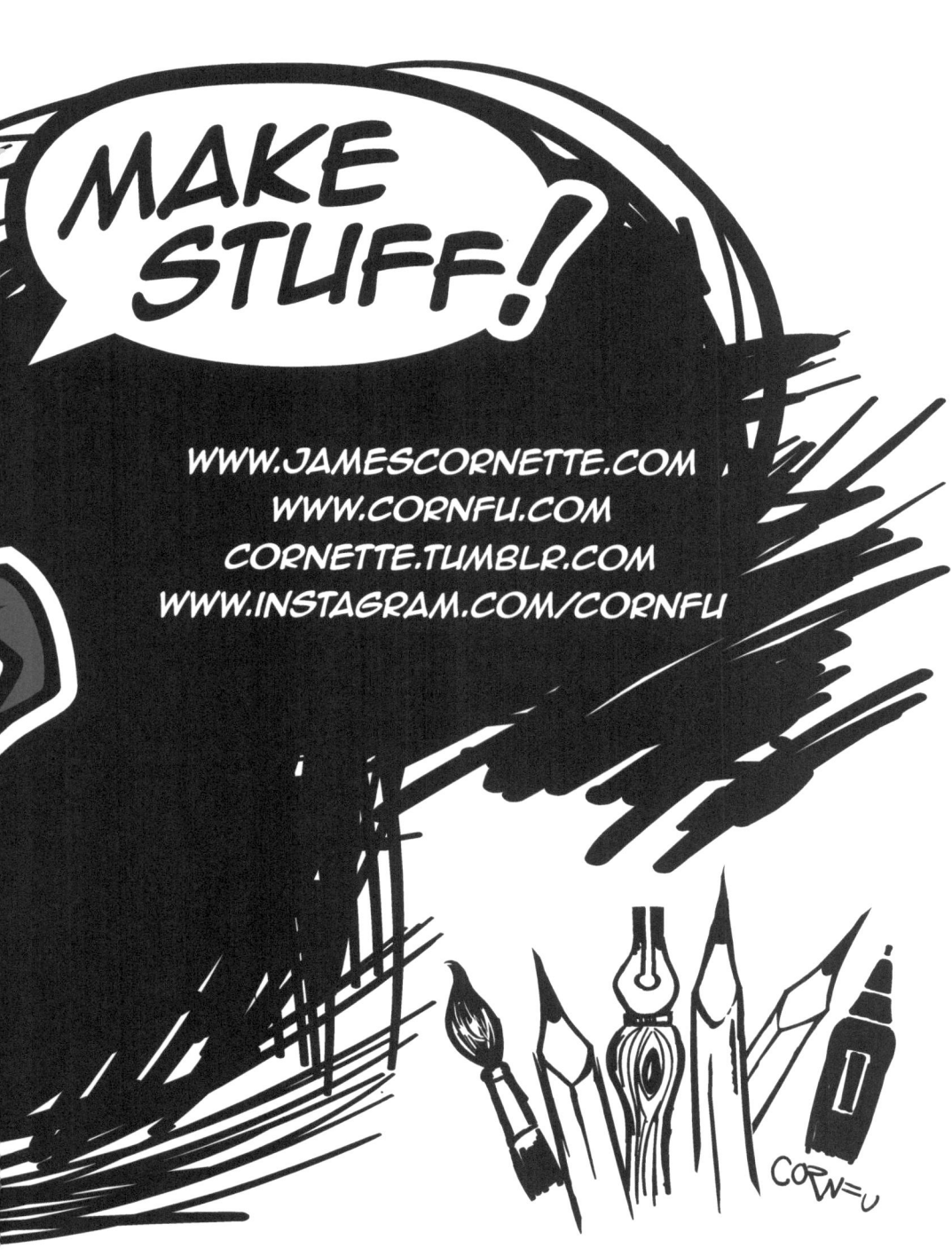

www.ingramcontent.com/pod-product-compliance
Lightning Source LLC
Chambersburg PA
CBHW041943240526
45473CB00033B/502